Be a TOP SCORER
in ISC Exams 2025

i Succeed

10 Sample Question Papers

with Quick Study Notes

English Language 12th

Paper 1

arihant
SUCCESS AND NOTHING LESS

Be a TOP SCORER
in ISC Exams 2025

i Succeed

10 Sample Question Papers

with Quick Study Notes

English Language 12th

Paper 1

AUTHOR
Navya Jain

List of *i* Succeed Sample Papers for ISC 12

- Physics
- Chemistry
- Maths
- Biology
- Accounts
- Economics
- Commerce
- English Language
- Literature in English

Arihant Prakashan
(School Division Series)

Administrative & Production Offices

Regd. Office
'Ramchhaya' 4577/15, Agarwal Road, Darya Ganj, New Delhi -110002
Tele: 011- 47630600, 43518550

Head Office
Kalindi, TP Nagar, Meerut (UP) - 250002
Tel: 0121-7156203, 7156204

Sales & Support Offices
Agra, Ahmedabad, Bengaluru, Bareilly, Chennai, Delhi, Guwahati, Hyderabad, Jaipur, Jhansi, Kolkata, Lucknow, Nagpur & Pune.

PRICE ₹175.00

PO No : TXT-XX-XXXXXXX-X-XX

Published by Arihant Publications (India) Ltd.

For further information about the books published by Arihant, log on to www.arihantbooks.com or e-mail at info@arihantbooks.com

Follow us on

i Succeed

SAMPLE QUESTION PAPERS

THE **BEST CHOICE** OF TEACHERS & STUDENTS, Why?

01 Exact Exam Pattern

All Sample Papers have been designed on the actual exam format of ISC

02 Complete Syllabus

Complete coverage of syllabus through different types of questions across all the sample papers

03 Latest Specimen Question Paper

Latest Specimen Question Paper with detailed answers.

04 Detailed Answers

Step-by-step answers to help you understand concepts and improve problem-solving skills.

05 All Type of Questions

Coverage of all type of exam pattern questions, writing tasks, grammar & reading comprehension.

Free Doubt Solving APP

To help you sort out your doubts at any time any place.

i Succeed

English Language 12

PREPARATION ASSESSMENT ZONE	**1-20**
ISC Specimen Paper	03-07
Answers	*07-11*
Board Exam Paper 2024	12-15
Answers	*15-19*
PROFICIENCY BUILDING ZONE	**21-104**
■ Sample Question Paper 1	23-26
Answers	*27-31*
■ Sample Question Paper 2	32-35
Answers	*36-39*
■ Sample Question Paper 3	40-43
Answers	*43-47*
■ Sample Question Paper 4	48-51
Answers	*51-55*
■ Sample Question Paper 5	56-59
Answers	*59-63*
■ Sample Question Paper 6	64-67
Answers	*67-72*
■ Sample Question Paper 7	73-76
Answers	*76-80*
■ Sample Question Paper 8	81-84
Answers	*84-88*
■ Sample Question Paper 9	89-92
Answers	*92-96*
■ Sample Question Paper 10	97-100
Answers	*100-104*

Course Structure
2024-25

PAPER I : THEORY 80 Marks

All questions will be compulsory

Question One : A composition on one of a number of subjects.

Question Two : (a) Directed writing.

(b) Proposal Writing based on a given situation.

Question Three : Short-answer questions to test grammar, structure and usage

Question Four : Comprehension.

Question One

Candidates will be required to select one composition topic from a choice of six. The choice will normally include narrative, descriptive, reflective, argumentative, discursive topics and original short story.

The required length of the composition is 400–450 words. The main criteria by which the compositions will be marked are as follows

(a) The quality of the language employed, the range and appropriateness of vocabulary and sentence structure, syntax, the correctness of grammatical constructions, punctuation and spelling.

(b) The degree to which candidates have been successful in organising the content of the composition as a whole and in individual paragraphs.

Question Two

There are two parts in this question and both parts are compulsory.

(a) **Directed Writing** The piece of directed writing must be based on the information and all the points provided. The required length is 250-300 words. The range of subjects includes feature article, book review, speech writing, newspaper report and statement of purpose. Skills such as amplifying, describing and re-stating are involved. The candidates' ability in the above skills, including format, will be taken into account as well as their ability to handle language appropriately in the context of the given situation.

(b) **Proposal Writing** Candidates will be required to write a proposal based on a given situation. The proposal should include

(i) An Introduction

(ii) Objectives

(iii) List of measures to be taken.

A concluding statement is necessary. The format prescribed by the CISCE must be followed. The candidates will also be marked on linguistic ability.

Question Three

All the items in this question are compulsory and their number and type / pattern may vary from year to year. They will consist of transformation of sentences, phrasal verbs, and verbs/tenses, which will test the candidates' knowledge of the essentials of functional English grammar and structure.

Question Four

A passage of about 700 words will be provided. Questions based on the passage will be as follows:

- Questions that test the candidates' analytical skills, knowledge of vocabulary, ability to understand the content, infer information and meanings from the text.
- A question that elicits the main ideas of all or part of the passage, where the candidate will be required to frame a summary (keeping to a word limit), in a coherent manner. Marks will be awarded for expression and the candidate's ability to summarise clearly in complete sentences. Marks will be deducted for linguistic errors.

NOTE: This part must be done in the grid form. Use of abbreviations and contractions will not be accepted.

Preparation Assessment Zone

Welcome to the Preparation Assessment Zone!

In this section, you'll find **ISC Specimen Question Paper** and **Board Examination Paper 2024** to help you assess your readiness. Attempt these papers to familiarise yourself with the exam format and identify areas that need improvement.

Progress Tracker **Tick the papers as you complete them.**

☐ ISC Specimen Paper

☐ Board Examination Paper 2024

ISC Specimen Paper

Session 2024-25

English Language (Code 801)

Class 12

General Instructions

1. You are allowed additional 15 minutes for only reading the question paper.
2. You must not start writing during reading time.
3. It has four questions in all.
4. Answer all questions.
5. You are advised to spend not more than 45 minutes on Question 1, 55 minutes on Question 2, 30 minutes on Question 3 and 50 minutes on Question 4.
6. You should begin each answer on a fresh page.
7. The intended marks for questions are given in brackets [ ].

Time Alloted : 3 Hrs.

Max. Marks : 80

Question 1.

Write a composition (in approximately 400-450 words) on **any one** of the following subjects. (20)

(You are reminded that you will be rewarded for the orderly and coherent presentation of the matter, use of appropriate style and general accuracy of spelling, punctuation and grammar.)

(i) You had to go on a train journey with your family. On reaching the railway station, you discovered that your train was delayed by two hours. Describe how you spent those two hours detailing what you saw, the sounds you heard, and the interactions you had with the people around you. Express your feelings when you saw the train finally approaching the station.

(ii) During the lunch break, a surprising sight unfolded as a monkey entered your school campus. Narrate your experience as you took charge and guided junior students to their classrooms ensuring their safety.

(iii) Parents should not influence their children when choosing the subjects they wish to study. Argue either **FOR** or **AGAINST** the given statement.

(iv) Life

(v) You become what you read. Present your reflections on this statement.

(vi) Write an original short story that ends with the following words: ...... when they realised that, sometimes, the most extraordinary stories begin with the simplest of moments.

Question 2.

(i) As the Head of Environmental Initiatives at school, you have to deliver a speech on the occasion of World Environment Day on 5th June. Write a speech following the guidelines given below. (15)

Greeting or salutation and purpose - the importance of World Environment Day - key issues such as climate change and pollution - the role of students in fostering a sense of environmental responsibility-concrete steps required towards a more sustainable and an eco-friendly lifestyle - strong call for action.

(ii) As the school leader, you have been given the responsibility of organising a school trip for the students of Classes XI and XII to a place of historical importance. Write a proposal in about 150 words stating the steps you would take to successfully organise the trip. (10)

Question 3.

Answer subparts **(i)**, **(ii)** and **(iii)**. (5)

(i) Rewrite the following sentences according to the instructions given after each of them in brackets.

(a) I don't know Helen very much; nevertheless, I like her.
(Begin: In spite of ....)

(b) They opened the window because they did not want the smoke to go into the kitchen.
(Use: so.... that)

(c) Chennai is bigger than most other Indian cities.
(End: .... Chennai.)

(d) He was so old that he could be my grandfather.
(Use...enough....)

(e) The judge said to the prosecutor, "Do you agree with the arguments presented yesterday"?
(Begin: The judge asked.....)

(ii) In the following sentences, replace the **INCORRECT** underlined words to make the sentences meaningful and grammatically correct. Do not copy the sentences. (5)

(a) The teacher handed <u>down</u> the report cards.

(b) She handed <u>in</u> the business to her son.

(c) The Minister gave <u>off</u> the prizes.

(d) The doctor gave <u>away</u> hope when she fell into a coma.

(e) I had to pull <u>over</u> a tough situation to meet the project deadline.

(f) When will the Shatabdi Express pull <u>up</u>?

(g) Some seats are set <u>by</u> for the handicapped.

(h) We immediately set <u>forth</u> fixing the roof.

(i) He ran <u>around</u> problems while trying to fix the computer.

(j) He ran <u>into</u> President during the elections last year.

(iii) Fill in the blanks in the passage given below with the appropriate form of the verb given in brackets. Do not write the passage but write the verbs in the correct order. (5)

Last summer, Emily had been working tirelessly on her garden. She.........**(1)** (plant) a variety of flowers, ... **(2)** (envision) a vibrant and colourful display. Every morning, she would spend hours tending to the blossoms ensuring they were thriving under the warm Sun.

One day, while she......... **(3)** (admire) her handiwork, she noticed a rare butterfly that had landed on one of the flowers. She had never seen such a beautiful specimen before. Excitedly, Emily ran into the house to grab her camera......... **(4)** (hope) to capture the fleeting moment.

By the time she returned, the butterfly......... **(5)** (fly) away. Disappointed, Emily......... **(6)** (realise) that she had missed the opportunity. However, the memory of that elusive butterfly lingered in her mind, and she decided......... **(7)** (create) a butterfly-friendly corner in her garden.

Months later, as Emily walked through her garden, she saw a familiar flutter of wings. The rare butterfly had returned, ... **(8)** (draw) by the blossoms that had bloomed since their last encounter. Grateful for the second chance, Emily .... **(9)** (capture) the moment on her camera cherishing the beauty that .... **(10)** (elude) her once before.

Question 4.

Read the passage given below and answer the questions (i), (ii) and (iii) that follow.

(1) "Can I see the Manager?" I said, and added solemnly, "Alone." I don't know why I said 'alone.' "Certainly," said the accountant and fetched him.

(2) The Manager was a grave, calm man. I held my fifty-six dollars clutched in a crumpled ball in my pocket. "Are you the Manager?" I asked. God knows I did not doubt it. "Yes," he said.

"Can I see you alone?" I asked.

(3) The Manager looked at me in some alarm. He felt that I had an awful secret to reveal.

"Come in here," he said and led the way to a private room. He turned the key in the lock.

"We are safe from interruption here," he said, 'sit down.'

We both sat down and looked at each other. I found no voice to speak.

"You are one of Pinkerton's men, I presume," he said.

(4) He had gathered from my mysterious manner that I was a detective. I knew what he was thinking, and it made me worse.

"No, not from Pinkerton's," I said, seeming to imply that I came from a rival agency. "To tell the truth," I went on as if I had been prompted to lie about it, "I am not a detective at all. I have come to open an account. I intend to keep all my money in this bank."

The Manager looked relieved but still serious; he concluded now that I was a son of Baron Rothschild or a young Gould.

"A large account, I suppose," he said.

"Fairly large," I whispered. "I propose to deposit fifty-six dollars now and fifty dollars a month regularly."

(5) The Manager got up and opened the door. He called to the accountant.

"Mr. Montgomery," he said unkindly loud, "this gentleman is opening an account, he will deposit fifty-six dollars. Good morning."

I rose. A big iron door stood open at the side of the room. "Good morning", I said and stepped into the safe. "Come out," said the Manager coldly and showed me the other way.

(6) I went up to the accountant's wicket and poked the ball of money at him with a quick convulsive movement as if I were doing a conjuring trick. My face was ghastly pale.

"Here," I said, "deposit it." The tone of the words seemed to mean, "Let us do this painful thing while the fit is on us."

He took the money and gave it to another clerk.

(7) He made me write the sum on a slip and sign my name in a book. I no longer knew what I was doing. The bank swam before my eyes.

"Is it deposited?" I asked in a hollow, vibrating voice.

"It is," said the accountant.

"Then I want to draw a cheque."

My idea was to draw out six dollars of it for present use. Someone gave me a chequebook through a wicket and someone else began telling me how to write it out. The people in the bank had the impression that I was an invalid millionaire. I wrote something on the cheque and thrust it in at the clerk. He looked at it.

(8) "What! Are you drawing it all out again?" he asked in surprise. Then, I realised that I had written fifty-six instead of six. I was too far gone to reason now. I had a feeling that it was impossible to explain the thing. I had burned my boats. All the clerks had stopped writing to look at me. Reckless with misery, I made a plunge.

"Yes, the whole thing."

"You withdraw all your money from the bank?"

"Every cent of it."

"Are you not going to deposit anymore?" said the clerk, astonished.

"Never."

(9) An idiot hope struck me that they might think something had insulted me while I was writing the cheque and that I had changed my mind. I made a wretched attempt to look like a man with a fearfully quick temper.

(10) The clerk prepared to pay the money.

"How will you have it?" he said. This question came as a bolt from the blue.

"What?"

"How will you have it?"

"Oh!" I caught his meaning and answered without even trying to think "in fifties."

He gave me a fifty-dollar bill.

"And the six?" he asked dryly.

"In sixes," I said.

He gave it to me and I rushed out.

As the big door swung behind me. I caught the echo of a roar of laughter that went up to the ceiling of the bank. Since then, I bank no more. I keep my money in cash in my trousers pocket and my savings in silver dollars in a sock. ***Adapted from:*** *My Financial Career By Stephen Leacock*

(i) (a) Find a single word from the passage that will exactly replace the underlined word or words in the following sentences. (3)

(1) The kind stranger <u>went and got back</u> the ball from where it had rolled into the bush.

(2) I took offence at the expression on his face that was clearly meant to <u>insinuate</u> I was a liar.

(3) The firm experienced a financial loss when the contract went to a <u>contender</u> who had just entered the business.

(b) For each of the words given below, choose the correct sentence that uses the same word unchanged in spelling but with a different meaning from that which it carries in the passage. (3)

(1) alarm (line 6)

(a) The silence from the other end set off alarm bells in her head.

(b) The pallor of his skin alarmed those standing around.

(c) I set my alarm for six o'clock but slept through it.

(d) The sound of the approaching jets caused some alarm in the war room.

(2) wicket (line 37)

(a) The wicketkeeper was the true saviour of the of the day for that one match.

(b) The team wanted to bat while the wicket was still dry.

(c) The man at the window handed us our tickets through the wicket.

(d) The quick loss of wickets demoralised the team.

(3) reason (line 41)

(a) After the tragedy, his ability to reason is severely diminished.

(b) They reasoned they could get better seats if they arrived early.

(c) Recipients of funds were selected without rhyme or reason.

(d) We have every reason to celebrate.

(ii) Answer the following questions as briefly as possible in your own words.

(a) With reference to the passage, explain the meaning of the expression of the 'I had burned my boats'. (2)

(b) Cite any two instances of the behaviour of the bank employees that indicate the insignificance of a deposit of fifty-six dollars. (2)

(c) Why do you think the people in the bank thought of the narrator as an 'invalid millionaire'? (2)

(iii) Summarise why the narrator decided to bank no more (paragraphs 6 to 10). You are required to write the summary in the form of a connected passage in about 100 words. Failure to keep within the word limit will be penalised. (8)

Answers *in Topper's Style*

1\. (i) Most of us often visit railway stations to travel or to receive or see off a friend or a relative. All of us would agree that the scene at a railway station is always attractive and colourful and full of diverse people and activities. There are people of various classes, regions and religions going about their task either waiting to pick someone up or to board a train.

A railway station is a meeting place for all sorts of people. I have always found myself observing the scene at the railway station whenever I visit it. But one particular day, at the railway station, stays with me forever. It was a normal day when I, along with my family, was travelling to a hill station during the holiday season from the train. We had arrived at the railway station with half an hour to the time pointed out in our tickets. However, on reaching the railway station, we discovered that our train was delayed by two hours and so we had to wait for some time. As usual, I started to look around to pass my time. There was usual hustle and bustle there. Everything seemed to be normal as one could around expect – the vendors' shouting, the passengers' anxiety, the coolies' handling the luggage of the passengers, etc.

After half an hour, an announcement was made wherein another train was arriving at the platform.
In a hurry, all the passengers started collecting their luggage. It was pure chaos and I was disturbed by the way people were pushing to get out of the train and get on the train. At the same time, there were coolies in red and khakhi attire offering tourists to carry their luggage. In a corner, you could also see vendors getting on and off the train to sell their wares.

The train stood on the platform for 15 minutes and then departed. All was quiet again and my siblings and I were getting bored. I asked my parents if I could buy some novels while my siblings wanted to buy some packed snacks. After much convincing, my parents agreed and I was taken to buy some books.
I bought 4 books and my siblings bought a ton of snacks.

I was sitting and reading one of the books when people again disassembled when the hoot of the train was heard nearby. This time my parents were collecting our luggage as it was our train. As the train stopped on the platform, people crowded the gates and started looking for their coaches again filling the railway station with its busy glory. We also hurried to board the train properly.

(ii) Have you ever come across a situation wherein you were at loss on what is to be done and there was complete chaos all around? Have you ever seen a sight of more than 200 students screaming and running here and there in the playground? Well, I have. My school is a place where students come from all across India and spend their schooling in the quaint hills of XYZ. As expected, my school is surrounded by forests which houses many animals including monkeys. There are high walls and various precautions taken by the school to avoid any problem with wild animals. But, sometimes, some animals come and create havoc. One such incident happened a few days back during lunch break.

My friends and I were sitting in the courtyard when we heard students screaming and running here and there in fear. Even teachers were scared and did not know what to do. When we went to see what was happening, we saw that a huge monkey had entered the school grounds and was snatching tiffin boxes from children. For a moment, we were struck with fear too; I do not really know what happened but, after a minute, I just calmly started rounding up children and getting them inside the building. While I was going around and getting children inside, one of my friends asked the peons to close all windows and doors expect one that was closest to me.

The ground was getting quieter as students realised that if they move calmly and quietly, the monkey would not harm them. Slowly and gradually, all students made a queue and entered the school building. The monkey was eating the food it has snatched from the children in the corner baring his teeth every once in a while.

It took us 20 minutes but we got all children inside and, by this time, the forest department had also arrived. They shot a tranquiliser at the monkey and, as the monkey slept, it was taken out to be freed far away from the school.

After this incident, the students were asked to gather in the courtyard wherein my friends and I were praised and students were told that they would be given a proper workshop on how to deal with such situations. For me, the day was weird as I had never imagined myself to be taking such a leadership role. But I guess, adversity brings out character.

(iii) **For the Motion**

Choosing the subject one wants to study, selecting a definite career and deciding a career goal is very important especially once you have completed your Sr. Sec. schooling. It helps in deciding one's future and is an essential first step in achieving one's goals. Unfortunately, not many students are able to discover their potential and interests, and that is when the pressure starts building up.

There is no denying the truth that, once we finish our school, we are faced with the question what next? A student at the threshold of a new start has elders, especially parents, acting as guides to help the child select a subject and path most suitable for them. However, I stand against this belief. I believe that parents should not influence their children when choosing the subjects they wish to study.

We need to understand that every child has the right to choose their career, and they have the right to live their dreams. Each individual has his/her strengths and weaknesses, aptitude, skills, performance and personality. As such, children are the only ones who truly know their interests, potential and abilities and, thus, can decide his or her career path quickly and aptly. This sets the path for not just self-awareness but also a path towards becoming a responsible and self-sustaining adult. Furthermore, it builds their confidence and strengthens their decision-making abilities.

While it does not mean that we should not listen to our elders, what I suggest is following one's own calling. If children choose a career according to their parents' wishes, they will have a boring academic life as they would face a lack of interest. It might even cause them to fail in their exams. They also would have to meet a lot of challenges and pressure which would negatively impact their future and confidence.

Thus, when students choose their subject and career that is well suited to their needs, they perform well and ultimately succeed in life. So, let us make an intelligent and professional move, and step ahead in the right direction with the help of those who are more aware and informed.

Thank you!

Against the Motion

Passing high school is crucial-what to do next – is even more critical. Making a right career choice involves a lot of thinking as you have to analyse various majors and right colleges. Today, most of the students are influenced by their parents while choosing a career and they end up on the path of success. Hence, I disagree with the statement that parents should not influence their children when choosing the subjects they wish to study.

It is true that a child knows his/her interests and potential better than anyone; but, he/she lacks experience in life. Parents can provide this experience, and through their knowledge, guide their children into opting for the subjects they should study; thus, opting for a suitable career. Furthermore, all parents want their children to find happiness and success in life. The right choice of a career will certainly provide happiness. Research in this field has indicated that, when children feel supported and loved by their parents, they have more confidence in their own ability to find a career that suits them and, therefore, choose one which will be interesting to them as well as provide them a livelihood. An individual should be the best judge to choose a career of his/her choice but he/she can seek guidance from parents and elders.

Career counsellors usually do not know anything about a child's personal interests before they suggest a career for him/her which may ultimately result in failure. They may fail in identifying a child's talents and even end up confusing them with multiple career options. Therefore, I reiterate that at parents should be able to influence their children when choosing the subjects they wish to study.

Thank you!

(iv) Life is a single word that encompasses many different connotations and meanings. It is more than just being alive; it's about how one defines existence. This aspect processes actions, and evolving through growth. Life is what distinguishes humans from inorganic matter.

As an enigmatic phenomenon, the concept and understanding of life has been a source of discourse for many. Philosophers, academics, poets and authors all around the world have written extensively about what it means to live and, more significantly, what are the essential elements that characterise one's existence.

While philosophers sought to understand the meaning and purpose of people's lives, poets and authors recorded the diversity of life at various times. However, for all of them, one thing remained constant- the meaning of life as the path or adventure of living. We are born, we live our lives and eventually we pass away with time. Hence, the concept of mortality is also associated with life.

One important aspect of life is that it keeps going forward. It doesn't stop with time and isn't hindered with any event in life. This means nothing is permanent. A happy occasion will come to pass, just like a sad one. There is a lot of stress all around us during the sad days. Most people complain about problems at office, issues in relationships and the growing competition in various fields. People are so engrossed in dealing with these issues that they forget to see the real beauty of life. They forget that one must be optimistic no matter how bad things get. Every situation, occasion and event, no matter how bad, shall pass.

In fact, if we look at life closely, we will realise how beautiful it is. God has given us an abundance of everything. This is evident when we look at the nature. The trees, plants, rivers and sunlight – everything is beautiful and in abundance and so is the energy that resides within us. This is the beauty of life.

However, this is not to say that life is a bed of roses. It is not! The problems and concerns of people are genuine. The rich, the poor, the educated, the uneducated, the beautiful and the not so beautiful – everyone has their own set of problems. Life is not easy for anyone. However, we need to understand that this is how life is. If everything came easy, we would not really value it. Life is beautiful in its own way, even with the problems, and it us upon us to look for reasons to enjoy it and embrace its beauty amid the issues we are dealing with.

(v) "It's in literature that true life can be found. It's under the mask of fiction that you can tell the truth", said Gao Xingjian.

Literature gives valuable insight into the true and hard facts of life which we can easily relate to and which makes us what we are today. It also inculcates virtues and the power of reasoning for, in the words of Francis Bacon, "Read not to contradict and confute nor to believe and take for granted, nor to find talk and discourse, but to weigh and consider."

The word 'literature' comes from the word 'letters' due to which learned men are often referred to as men of letters. The literary work of great authors influence us immensely and make up our ideas and belief systems. Since time immemorial, great literary works like the *Vedas*, the *Ramayana*, the *Gita*, the *Bible* and the *Koran* spread the light of truth and wisdom in the world. The *Ramayana* presents valuable insight into human relationships like respect for elders and behaviour towards relatives, friends and colleagues.

The *Gita* idolised Karma (duty) which is the purpose of life. Such books provide strength and inspiration in times of crisis or when faced with a dilemma. They are indeed masterpieces that unfold the truth of life and death making one reverent, yet fearless. Besides this, the classics of William Shakespeare, Rabindra Nath Tagore, Munshi Premchand, etc. bequeathed to us a wealth of knowledge on aspects like friendship, virtues, honesty and life itself.

Reading such literature impacts our lives profoundly. Besides providing valuable insight into the good and positive aspects of life, it also makes us aware of the pitfalls that result from wrong doings. The true-to-life portrayal of characters enables one to differentiate between good or bad, virtue and vice. This realisation makes one more humane and virtuous. Unfortunately, the youth do not prefer to read books except those prescribed in their syllabus. This is because of the overpowering influence of other media like television, cinema and the Internet.

Besides developing the personality, reading inculcates good morals and family values, which are extremely important for living a wholesome life. It improves one's quality of life and makes one think and act logically thereby resolving many life problems. Many such problems are overcome by the direction and strength derived from the literary work of great sages.

Undoubtedly, literary works of great authors impact our lives profoundly. Their inspiring thoughts, besides broadening our vision, also make us more worldly wise by adding a new dimension to our personality. Indeed, in the words of Boris Pasternak, "Literature is the art of discovering something extraordinary about ordinary people and saying with ordinary words something extraordinary."

(vi) The graveyard was cold, dark and dreary. One weary old oak tree leaned over the entrance gate and broken, battered headstones were scattered all around. He could hear the sound of the howling wind and the creak and groan of branches as they swayed in the mysterious night. He was scared but he knew that he had to do this. The smell of fear and rotting leaves filled his nostrils and he breathed deeply afraid that he would get sick. As he walked towards the grave, he heard another noise. It was of slow heavy footsteps. When he turned around, he saw police officer Jay walking towards him. "I don't think this is a good idea", he shouted. "It's too late to change your mind", Captain Jay replied in a low threatening voice. "Either we dig him up now or the mystery remains unsolved."

"Ok, Ok", he mumbled.

Mohak could never forget the scare he had when he got to know that his neighbour had died in mysterious circumstances. As a failed author, he had shared his grievances about lack of inspiration to his dear old neighbour who would grumble but still listen attentively. The death, according to the reports, was unnatural but the police had no lead. Mohak knew something was fishy for the old man was fit, too fit for his age, and he could not just die like that. Hence, he took the matter in his own hands. When he found Captain Jay following him, they both decided to solve the case together.

Now, they were at a graveyard. Mohak leaned heavily with the dusty shovel in his hands and started to dig, determined to uncover the truth. Jay also began to dig at the other end of the grave and soon they could see the coffin. Faced with this moment of truth, Mohak began to panic. What if he was wrong? What if he was disturbing a grave for no reason? After mustering much courage, he finally opened the coffin and saw that the corpse did not resemble his neighbour. Both the men were shook. If Mohak's neighbour had died, where was his body? What happened to the old man? How would they find his body?

Vijay stopped writing his weekly story leaving the readers at a cliffhanger. Nobody knew how Vijay could come up with such a story. It was only after Vijay had talked about his neighbour and his journey as a police officer when they realised that, sometimes, the most extraordinary stories begin with the simplest of moments.

2. (i) Good Morning Respected Principal, honourable teachers and dear friends.

Today I, Rishabh Shukla, the Head of Environmental Initiatives at School, stand before all of you on the occasion of World Environment Day. Designated by the UN Assembly, 5th June is celebrated as the World Environment Day (WED) to create an awareness about the kind of environment we are living in, and the need to conserve and preserve it for the present and the future. However, I feel sorry for all of us as I stand here to speak about how we all are putting our existence at risk with the ever increasing pollution as well as impact of climate change and what we can do to reduce it.

Pollution and climate change are the biggest challenges that humanity is facing as they directly affects our lives. The human existence can come under threat if pollution level increases to a hazardous level. In fact, if we talk about the present, the wildfires, pandemics, hurricanes, droughts, floods and many other effects can already be seen on a daily basis.

Pollution and climate change impact our lives negatively. Hence, we need to find ways to curb it and implement them immediately. Students can play a key role in helping to reduce pollution and create a healthy atmosphere for us to live in without fearing for our health. For instance, we can contribute to reducing the emission of harmful gases by either walking or cycling to school. We can also lead anti-pollution campaigns, tree plantation drives, be careful in the use of electricity and stop participating in activities that cause pollution.

By taking concrete steps required towards a more sustainable and an eco-friendly lifestyle, students can play their role as sensible citizens by fostering a sense of environmental responsibility.

The understanding of the dangers of pollution has to start at a young age as students especially are well poised to live a life that is pollution-free as well as to spread awareness on the importance of a safe future. It is time to take a strong stand and strive towards a promising existence.

Thank you!

(ii) **Proposal for Organising a Trip to a Historically Important Place**

Heading To foster an interest in the history of the nation and to introduce the students of Classes XI and XII to the historical integrity, splendor and tradition of the nation while providing an opportunity to engage with history firsthand.

Objectives The trip to a place of historical importance would help students learn about our past, cultural heritage, and the significance of events that have shaped our society. It would foster a deeper cultural understanding and empathy towards people from different backgrounds and periods, laying the foundation for a more harmonious and inclusive society.

List of Measures

- An appropriate destination will be selected after careful consideration with all the teachers.
- A Tourism firm will be contacted to make a budget-friendly package for the selected destination.
- The package selected will include lodgings, food, tourism and some fun activities.
- Then, a circular with all details will be provided to students with the deadline.
- It will be decided that we will take 1 teacher for every 15 students so that the management could be effective.

We hope that the proposal will be accepted so that the trip can be organised well.

3. (i) (a) In spite of not knowing Helen very much, I like her.
(b) They opened the window so that the smoke would not go into the kitchen.
(c) Very few Indian cities are as big as Chennai.
(d) He was old enough to be my grandfather.
(e) The judge asked the prosecutor if he agreed with the arguments presented the previous day.

(ii) (a) out (b) over (c) away (d) up
(e) through (f) in (g) aside (h) about
(i) into (j) for

(iii) (1) had planted (2) envisioning (3) was admiring (4) hoping
(5) had flown (6) realised (7) to create (8) drawn
(9) captured (10) had eluded

4. (i) (a) (1) fetched (2) imply (3) rival
(b) (1) (c) I set my alarm for six o'clock but slept through it.
(2) (b) The team wanted to bat while the wicket was still dry.
(3) (d) We have every reason to celebrate.

(ii) (a) The given expression 'I had burned my boats' means deciding or taking an action that makes it impossible to return to the previous situation. It essentially signifies that the narrator could not go back on his decision.
(b) Two instances of the behaviour of the bank employees that indicate the insignificance of a deposit of fifty-six dollars are
- When the narrator was withdrawing the amount, the clerk sarcastically asked the denomination in which he wanted it.
- The narrator's exit was followed by a roar of laughter.

(c) The people in the bank thought of the narrator as an 'invalid millionaire' because the narrator was nervous. At the accountant's window, he grew pale and his movements became convulsive. As he wrote and signed his name, he became even more nervous and his voice became hollow. When the cheque book was handed to him, somebody tried explaining how to write it out since it was obvious. He was physically distressed and fumbling.

(iii)

The	narrator	wanted	to	open
an	account	with	fifty-six	dollars.
The	manager	coldly	instructed	the
accountant	to	help	him.	The
narrator	unsteadily	passed	on	his
money	to	the	accountant	who
passed	it	to	the	clerk.
The	narrator	had	to	write
the	sum	down	and	sign.
He	asked	to	make	a
withdrawal	intending	to	withdraw	six
dollars.	In	his	agitation,	he
withdrew	the	entire	sum.	He
could	not	reason	or	explain
his	action	so	recklessly	stated
that	he	was	withdrawing	the
entire	amount	he	had	deposited.

(Candidates must write the precis in a grid. Exceeding of word limit will be penalised.)

Board Exam Paper 2024

Session 2024-25

English Language (Code 801)

Class 12

General Instructions

1. Candidates are allowed additional 15 minutes for only reading the paper. They must **Not** start writing during this time.
2. Attempt all four questions
3. The intended marks for questions or parts of questions are given in brackets [ ].

(You are advised to spend not more than 45 minutes on Question 4)

- No. of Questions : 4
- Time Alloted : 3 Hrs.
- Max. Marks : 80

Question 1.

Write a composition (in approximately 400-450 words) on **any one** of the following subjects. (20)

(You are reminded that you will be rewarded for the orderly and coherent presentation of the matter, use of appropriate style and general accuracy of spelling, punctuation and grammar.)

(i) Recently, you attended the wedding of a close relative. It was the first family gathering after the pandemic. Describe the excitement of meeting all the family members, the venue of the wedding, the food that was served and the celebrations that followed.

(ii) During the summer break, you joined a group of young people who read to the elderly at a senior citizens' home. Narrate your experience of reading to the elderly and the interactions you had with them. How did this experience impact you?

(iii) Cooking should be made a compulsory subject in the higher classes. Argue either **FOR** or **AGAINST** the given statement.

(iv) Music

(v) A person should be judged by the way they treat their subordinates. Present your reflections on this statement.

(vi) Write an original short story that begins with the following words.

"She was still on the phone giving out instructions when…"

Question 2.

(i) Write a review of a film that you watched recently, using the points given below. (15)

The review is to be published in your school newsletter and should not exceed 300 words.

Name of the film and director–lead actors and their performances–plot–setting–description of a scene that you particularly liked - rating and recommendation.

(ii) As a Member of the Student Council of ABC School, you wish to start a Laughter Club to develop the appreciation for humour among students. Write a proposal in not more than 150 words outlining the steps you would take to make this club a success. (10)

Question 3.

Answer sections **(i)**, **(ii)** and **(iii)**. (5)

(i) In each of the following items, sentence I is complete, while sentence **II** is not.

Complete sentence **II** making it is similar as possible to sentence **I.** Write sentence **II** in each case.

Example:

(z) (I) The heavy showers of rain revived the plants.

(II) The plants ....

Ans. (z) The plants were revived by the heavy showers of rain.

(a) (I) P. G. Wodehouse is the funniest author I have ever read.

(II) No other ....

(b) (I) Michelangelo was an architect and a poet.

(II) Not only ....

(c) (I) Sara said that she would come to my house the following day.

(II) Sara said to me,"...........

(d) (I) As soon as the students enter their classroom, the teacher welcomes them.

(II) No sooner ....

(e) (I) Only the wearer knows where the shoe pinches.

(II) None ....

(ii) Fill in each blank with a suitable word. (Do not write the sentence.) (5)

(a) We must carry .... despite the challenges we come across.

(b) The police promised to carry .... a thorough investigation.

(c) He is sure to appeal .... the judgement since it was unfavourable to him.

(d) The leader appealed .... the public to maintain law and order.

(e) The experienced doctor found it easy to deal .... young patients.

(f) This particular shop deals .... organic food.

(g) The fresh college graduate jumped .... the first offer of a job.

(h) My mother advised me never to jump .... conclusions.

(i) The signboard in the park read 'Keep .... the lawn'.

(j) It is not easy to keep ....with the rapidly changing fashions.

(iii) Fill in the blanks in the passage given below with the appropriate form of the verb given in brackets. Do not write the passage but write the verbs in the correct order. (5)

A young man had a beautiful garden in his mansion. As he loved flowers, shrubs and trees, he tended to the garden himself. Next to his mansion, there was a small house in which .... **(1)** (live) an old man. One day, when the young man was .... **(2)** (expect) some special guests, he took extra care in .... **(3)** (tend) to the garden. He pulled the weeds, ... **(4)** (trim) the shrubs, combed the moss and spent a long time meticulously .... **(5)** (rake) up and carefully arranging all the dry autumn leaves. As he worked, the old man .... **(6)** (watch) him with interest from across the wall that .... **(7)** (separate) their houses.

When he had finished, the young man stood back to .... **(8)** (admire) his work. "Isn't it beautiful?", he called out to the old man. "Yes", replied the old man, "but there is something missing. Help me over this wall and I'll put it right for you."

After a slight hesitation, the young man .... **(9)** (lift) the old fellow over and set him down. Slowly, the old man walked to the tree near the centre of the garden, grabbed it by the trunk and shook it. Leaves .... **(10)** (shower) down all over the garden and formed a beautiful carpet. 'There', said the old man, "now it is perfect!"

Question 4.

Read the passage given below and answer the questions (i), (ii) and (iii) that follow.

(1) The Police Superintendent is walking across the market square followed by a constable. Suddenly, he hears a loud shout, "So you bite, you damned brute? Lads, don't let the dog go! Biting is prohibited nowadays!"

There is the sound of yelping and the Superintendent sees a dog running out of a timber-yard. A man runs after it and tries to seize the dog by its hind legs. Sleepy countenances protrude from the shops and soon a crowd gathers.

(2) "It looks like a <u>row</u>, your honour", says the constable.

The Superintendent turns to his <u>left</u> and strides towards the crowd. He sees the aforementioned man standing close by the gate of the timber-yard, holding his right hand in the air and displaying a bleeding finger to the crowd. He was the town's goldsmith. The culprit who has caused the sensation, a white puppy with a sharp muzzle and a yellow patch on its back, is sitting on the ground.

"What's it all about?", the Superintendent inquires pushing his way through the crowd, "Who was it that shouted?"

(3) The goldsmith answers, "I was walking along here not interfering with anyone when this low brute, for no rhyme or reason, bit my finger. I am a working man.

Mine is fine work. I must have damages for I shan't be able to use this finger for a week."

(4) "I won't let this pass! Find out whose dog it is and draw up a report!", the Superintendent commands the constable.

(5) "I <u>fancy</u> it's General Zhigalov's dog", says someone in the crowd.

Suddenly indignant, the Superintendent turns to the goldsmith and asks, "There's one thing I can't make out. How could it have bitten you? Surely, it couldn't reach your finger. It's a little dog, and you are a great hulking fellow! You must have scratched your finger with a nail and then the idea struck you to get damages for it. I know your sort!"

(6) "No, that's not the General's dog", says the constable, with profound conviction, "the General has valuable dogs and goodness knows what this is! No coat, no shape, a low creature."

The Superintendent says, "You have been injured, goldsmith and we can't let the matter drop. You must be compensated for the damage."

(7) "It is the General', that's certain!", says a voice in the crowd.

"Oh! Constable, take the dog to the General's and enquire there. Say I found it and sent it. And tell them not to let it out into the street. A dog is a delicate animal. And you, you goldsmith, put your hand down. It's your own fault."

On seeing the General's cook approaching the superintendent asks him, "Is it one of yours?"

"We have never had one like this", says the cook.

"There's no need to waste time asking", decides the superintendent "It's a stray dag. Chase it away!"

(8) "It's not our dog", the cook goes on, "it belongs to the General's brother who arrived the other day."

"Is his Excellency's brother here? Delighted to hear it," says the Superintendent, and his whole face beams with an ecstatic smile, "it's not a bad pup. A lively creature, indeed. Come, why are you shivering, you nice little pup?"

(9) The cook calls the dog and walks away from the timber-yard.

(10) The crowd laughs at the goldsmith.

Adapted from : *A Chameleon by Anton Chekov*

(i) (a) Given below are three words and phrases. Find the words which have a similar meaning in the passage. (3)

(1) faces

(2) walks purposefully

(3) precious

(b) For each of the words given below, choose the sentence that uses the same word **unchanged in form, but with a different meaning** from that which it carries in the passage. (3)

(1) row (line 7)

(a) We sat in a row at the back of the room.

(b) My brother and I were having a row when our father arrived.

(c) A row has broken out amongst the vendors.

(d) The fisherman rowed us back to the shore.

(2) left (line 8)

(a) I instructed the driver to take a left turn at the intersection.

(b) The bank is situated to the left of the library.

(c) They left the house at six o'clock in the morning to reach the airport on time.

(d) He's giving away money left, right and centre.

(3) fancy (line 20)

(a) He fancies himself as a serious actor.

(b) I was foot-loose and fancy-free in those days.

(c) He had some fanciful notion about crossing the Atlantic in a barrel.

(d) He sells poor goods but charges fancy prices.

(ii) Answer the following questions in your own words as briefly as possible.

(a) How does power play an important role in the Superintendent's decisions? (2)

(b) Why does the goldsmith ask for damages? (2)

(c) Who does the dog belong to? How do we know it? (2)

(iii) Trace the Superintendent's reactions from the time the initial voice in the crowd is heard till the cook takes the dog away (paragraphs 5 to 9). You are required to write the summary in the form of a connected passage in about 100 words. Failure to keep within the word limit will be penalised. (8)

Answers *in Topper's Style*

1. (i) The COVID - 19 pandemic that hit the whole world in 2020 has left a distinct mark on everyone's life. We had to stay indoors and the only people we could see were our family members. It was a challenging time for each one of us. As someone who enjoys spending time with like-minded people, it was frustrating to stay cooped up at home.

As luck would have it, my cousin Ankita's marriage got fixed and it took place last month. I was on cloud nine as it was the first-ever function I attended after the Covid lockdown. I couldn't contain my elation at the thought of finally reuniting with my cousins and relatives after such a long time of not seeing each other physically.

The wedding was a grand celebration as Ankita is the first person in my generation from the paternal side of our family to get married. As the eldest child of the whole family, she is adored and loved by all. The wedding was held in the Hotel Seven Seas in North Delhi. The venue was adorned luxuriously with lights, candles, diyas and flamboyant flowers. The bride and groom chose pastel-themed wedding attires and both of them looked stunning. There were videos being played, on the big screen, of the bride and groom's childhood and teenage years. We went around taking pictures with every near and dear one.

The best part of the function has got to be the food served there. It ranged from sweet, sour, spicy to tangy delicacies. There were starters, main course and desserts which varied from vegetarian to non-vegetarian. In order to respect the attendees' choices, the vegetarian and non-vegetarian sections were set out in different areas. Out of everything, the desserts were my favourite. I still can't get over the taste of the chocolate truffle that just melted in my mouth.

After the wrapping up of the garland exchange and other rituals, there was a DJ party for the youngsters and a ghazal event for the elderly. I danced and sang along with my cousins and enjoyed myself to the fullest. The wedding concluded with appreciation speeches from the parents of the groom and the bride to the attendees. It was a one of a kind wedding function and the best one that I have ever attended. All in all, it was a grandiose wedding.

(ii) Having gone through the experience of interacting with the elderly on a daily basis, my views on the world have changed drastically. As a person in the prime of my life, I often found spending time with my elders boring and exhausting as I felt that all they did was nag and give unsolicited advice. I have noticed that this is the preconceived opinion that all youngsters including myself seem to have. I couldn't have been more wrong.

Last summer vacation, one of my cousins, who often visits a senior citizens' home, suggested that I volunteer there as they were short on people to assist the elderly for some activities. I was reluctant at first but, upon further reflection, agreed to the proposal. What made me change my mind is that all I had to do was read to the elderly. As an avid reader and someone who loves to share my reading experiences with others, that just appeared like a perfect opportunity.

On the first day, I met with the elderly at the home and noted down their likes and dislikes. Much to my surprise, they were quite active and welcomed me wholeheartedly. The time allotted was two hours for this session. I was overwhelmed with the undivided attention received from the elderly while I was reading the books. They would ask questions in a polite manner and, from time to time, shared experiences, folktales and stories from the past which they thought might interest me. They also always made sure to ask if I had eaten or was enjoying the time spent with them. Never once did they talk down to me because I am a youngster or tried to brush off my perspectives on certain things as mere immature thoughts. Their thoughtfulness, down-to-earth and caring nature made me realise that we should never be prejudiced against anyone.

The most heartbreaking thing I learned from this experience was that the elders were abandoned by their own children whom they had nurtured and provided for. However, neither had they complained nor spoken ill about their children. Instead, they were satisfied with how they found happiness because of their children. I couldn't wrap my head around it initially but, with time, I realised that it was because the elderly have so much love to give to the world.

All in all, volunteering and spending time with the elderly has been the best decision I have ever made in my life and I am planning to visit them whenever I can. I have started spending more time with the elders at my home, and less time on phone and games. I take an oath to myself to never let my parents and grandparents be in the kind of situation as the ones in a senior citizens' home.

(iii) **For the Motion**

It is important for a person to learn basic life skills from an appropriate age and time in order to become an independent and competent individual in life. One such life skill is cooking. Unfortunately, it is often overlooked and deemed as a non-requirement by most people. Students usually opt for ready-made meals and junk food that have extremely low nutritional value and are laden with harmful fats, calories, sugar and salts. Hence, I stand in favour of the motion cooking should be made a compulsory subject in the higher classes.

Learning how to cook enhances one's thinking, analytical, budgeting and time management skills. The planning of the ingredients requires one to assess different nutrient requirements of people in various stages of their life cycle. It is found that people who frequently engage in baking sessions develop better self-esteem as a result of their improved concentration, coordination and confidence. Another advantage is that one will be able to adapt in any environment properly as they will have developed a self-sufficient lifestyle and the ability to appreciate diversity in food.

There is an underlying social importance in learning cooking. It is one skill that is often seen as a task delegated to women in our male-dominated society. Teaching the students of higher classes who already have the ability to pick out rights from wrongs will help in breaking this stereotype.

Cooking can also lead a person to their future career path. When a student is exposed to cooking and baking from a younger age, there is a possibility to uncover hidden abilities in culinary art. There is the potential for students to pursue a career in the ever-booming global hospitality and catering industry.

Cooking should be considered as an art just like any other activity which requires skills and expertise. It is important that schools impart the students with knowledge of preparing healthy meals and help the students grow up as healthy and responsible adults.

Hence, taking into account the practical and social notability of acquiring cooking skill, it should be made a compulsory subject in the higher classes in every school.

Against the Motion

Many schools have started to introduce cooking classes as part of the school curriculum. Cooking is indeed one survival skill that everyone must acquire. However, as it is known, the academic curriculum set up by education board is heavy and students already have quite a tight schedule. In higher classes, the number of subjects and topics to be learned is already increased manifold. The question now lies in whether it is suitable for cooking to be taught in school and I stand against the motion.

It should be taken into consideration that organising and conducting cooking classes might be cumbersome. On top of the cooking equipments being costly, they also occupy a large space. This means that each of the classes for which the cooking class is made mandatory will need separate classrooms designed specifically in order to include the students and equip all the materials required. There will also be the problem of not having enough trained staffs to teach and help the students. As most of the students would be new to it, there is a high chance of ingredients getting wasted unnecessarily and accidents due to the burners or ovens.

As cooking is a relatively easy task, it can be learned at home and it is the responsibility of the parents to prepare the students for life outside of education. One can start learning by the trial and error method. Family members are also present at home to assist in case one needs help with anything. In addition to that, all the information about different kinds of cooking methods and ways to prepare food is easily available on the internet. There is no hard and fast rule that says that every life skill must only be imparted at school. We should leave enough room to learn different things at home.

Therefore, as schools already have the responsibility of preparing the students cognitively for a working life, introducing cooking as a compulsory subject in the higher classes is not appropriate.

(iv) **Music**

The word 'music' is quite nuanced and can be defined in many ways according to different perspectives and ideas. The word originated from the Greek word 'mousike' which translates to 'Art of the Muses'. The Muses in Greek mythology were the Goddesses who inspired the arts such as literature, music and poetry. And its definitions can vary from practical and theoretical to philosophical.

The history of music can be traced back to pre-historic times as humans possess an inherent passion to express emotions through the medium of music. It is predicted that the human voice might have been the first musical idea which took a concrete form. In due course, all the existing cultures developed musical instruments so as to produce greater variety in musical expression. These various musical expressions were used to serve purposes such as religious rituals, entertainment, important events and as healing art. It was prominent in the ancient cultures of China, Africa, Greece, the Americas, Egypt and India.

Music is an essential feature of culture and society which interlink individuals. Each culture and every period of time has its own popular music style. The style may be drastically different or parallel of each other. Whatever the style may be, it can stimulate people to social change and invoke age-old traditions. It is also observed that different cultures highlight different musical instruments or techniques.

Musical instruments are simply defined as devices that are used to create sound. It is believed that the first musical instruments were human bodies. People in ancient times used to produce sound by clapping and creating vocal expressions. With time, musical instruments were developed and one form expanded into other forms. In modern times, musical instruments are classified on the basis of their physical properties, how music is performed on the instrument, how sound is produced, the range of the instrument, and the instrument's place in an orchestra or other ensembles. The commonly known classification includes stringed instruments (guitar, violin, piano), wind instruments (flute, saxophone, harmonium), percussion instruments of wood or metal (chimes, xylophone) and percussion instruments with skin heads (tambourine, drum).

Music is considered as an art for healing. In contemporary world, it is often infused in the treatment process of various disorders. This process is referred to as music therapy. This is because listening to music that one loves results in the release of dopamine and oxytocin in the brain.

In conclusion, music is a universal language and can be found outside and within everything in nature. Music, above all, works in sound and time. It is a communication just like speech which requires us to listen, process and respond.

(v) The statement 'A person should be judged by the way they treat their subordinates' encapsulates a fundamental aspect of ethical leadership and interpersonal relationships. We often say that treating others regardless of their social, economic and monetary standing is a sign of utmost respect. Well, practising it should be the norm in order to create an equal and respectable society where people don't feel discriminated.

The way someone treats their subordinates often reflects their character and values. Respect, empathy and fairness in interactions with subordinates demonstrate integrity and a commitment to equal treatment of others regardless of hierarchical differences. Treating an ordinary sweeper as well as a prestigious CEO (Company Executive Officer) with the same respect exemplifies how you behave equally with everyone and also shows strong moral character. The behaviour towards subordinates sheds light on how individuals wield their power and authority. Compassionate and supportive leadership fosters a positive work environment, encourages collaboration and empowers employees to contribute their best efforts. On the other hand, mistreatment or abuse of power creates toxic dynamics, dissolves trust and undermines organisational morale.

People who conduct themselves respectfully towards others serve as role models whose actions set the tone for the entire society. When individuals prioritise respectful and inclusive treatment of subordinates, it sets a precedent for others to follow, fostering a culture of mutual respect, open communication and shared accountability. But, when individuals exhibit disdain or disregard for their subordinates, it can sustain a culture of fear, resentment and disengagement.

In the professional world, the way subordinates are treated directly influences their well-being, job satisfaction and performance. Employees who feel valued, supported and respected by their superiors are more likely to be motivated, productive and committed to organisational goals. Toxic leadership, on the contrary can lead to increased stress and burnout among employees, negatively impacting their overall performance.

The way a person treats their subordinates can have everlasting implications on their reputation and overall relationship with society. People who prioritise building positive relationships and nurturing lesser confident people are more likely to be remembered and respected for their contributions to the society. Conversely, people who engage in abusive or shameful behaviour may face repercussions, tarnishing their reputation and diminishing their respect over time.

In conclusion, how individuals treat their subordinates speaks volumes about their character, leadership style and commitment to fostering healthy interpersonal relationships. By maintaining principles of respect, fairness and empathy in their interactions with subordinates, people can cultivate a culture of mutual trust, collaboration and excellence that benefits both individuals and society in the long run.

(vi) She was still on the phone giving out instructions when there was a sudden jerk and she almost fell out of her seat in the car. She was startled and was ready to reprimand the driver when she saw a commotion outside. As she had urgent business to take care of at the office, she urged the driver to check out the issue and to leave as soon as possible. The driver went outside and didn't return for a good fifteen minutes or so; she was feeling jittery as she couldn't miss the meeting that day. After some time, the driver returned and, to her absolute horror, informed her that the road would be blocked for at least an hour.

Upon inspection, it was found that three road rollers malfunctioned at the same time and crashed on a pillar of the over-bridge which resulted in blocking the road. There wasn't enough space for even a bike a go through. Fortunately, there wasn't any casualty but all the vehicles that were travelling by that road had to line up and stay put for an hour. Furthermore, it was a one-way road so the chance of swerving to another lane was out of the window.

After collecting her thoughts, she called her subordinates to inform of the incident. Surprisingly, none of them picked up her call. She then tried calling the reception; still, no one received the call on the other side. Initially, she assumed that it might be her network problem so she tried from the driver's phone. When she couldn't connect with the other side, she started getting confused. She couldn't think of any reason why no one in the office had got back to her despite calling and texting multiple times. She decided to wait and enquire about it once she reached her office.

After waiting for an hour, which felt like an eternity to her, they were able to drive away. Upon reaching her office, to her utter shock, she found out that a fire had brokenout in the office building. The whole building was caught on fire and there were many casualties. Since there was a blackout before the fire, several people inside the building couldn't be evacuated on time. The floor in which she worked had the most number of injured people. Only when had she calmed herself down did she realise that the commotion from earlier had actually saved her from such a misfortune.

2. (i) *

(ii) **Proposal for Starting a Laughter Club**

Heading To develop appreciation for humour among students so as to provide a healthy space for them to freely express themselves.

Objectives The Laughter Club would be primarily introduced with the aim of promoting physical, mental and emotional well-being of the students of ABC School.

List of Measures

- The club will need a separate room with little furniture and enough space for students to sit in a circle in the middle.
- Any student from Classes VIII to XII can apply for the membership of the club.
- The club sessions and activities will be set up outside of class hours so as to not hinder the students' studies.
- Teachers would be requested to participate in some of the activities.
- Entry fee will be 100 ₹ per student which is to be kept as fund.

We hope that the proposal will be accepted so that the Laughter Club can be established officially.

3. (i) (a) No other author that I have read is as funny as P.G. Wodehouse.

(b) Not only was Michelangelo an architect but also a poet.

(c) Sara said to me, "I will come to your house tomorrow."

(d) No sooner had the students entered their classroom than the teacher welcomed them.

(e) None but the wearer knows where the shoe pinches.

(ii) (a) on (b) out (c) to (d) to
(e) with (f) with (g) on (h) to
(i) off (j) up

(iii) (1) lived (2) expecting (3) tending (4) trimmed
(5) raking (6) watched (7) separated (8) admire
(9) lifted (10) showered

4. (i) (a) (1) faces – countenances (2) walks purposefully–strides
(3) precious – valuable

(b) (1) (a) We sat in a row at the back of the room.
(2) (c) They left the house at six o'clock in the morning to reach the airport on time.
(3) (d) He sells poor goods but charges fancy prices.

(ii) (a) Power plays a huge role in the Superintendent's decisions. When he finds out that the goldsmith has been bitten by a dog, he is ready to find its owner and write a report regarding the incident. However, as soon as someone mentions that the dog could be General Zhigalov's, he changes his side and puts the blame on the goldsmith instead.

(b) The goldsmith asks for damages because his finger is bleeding due to the dog's bite and he won't be able to use that finger for a week. Since he needs his fingers in perfect shape to be able to earn his bread and butter, he asks for compensation.

(c) The dog belongs to the General's brother. Upon asking the General's cook when he/she reaches the timber-yard, it is found that the dog is not the General's but his brother's who arrived few days back.

(iii) The Superintendent changes his reactions like how chameleon changes its colour. When someone says that the dog might be General Zhigalov's, he suddenly becomes disgruntled towards the goldsmith. He accuses him of hurting himself and blaming it on the dog to get reparation. However, when the constable pronounces that the dog is not the General's, he starts to sympathise with the goldsmith. He keeps on changing sides till he finds out it belongs to the General's brother. His whole demeanour changes and he treats the dog as a precious being; thus, deciding to join in the more powerful side.

**This has been removed from latest syllabus 2024-25.*

Proficiency Building Zone

Welcome to the Proficiency Building Zone !

This section contains **10 Sample Question Papers** designed to enhance your problem-solving skills and proficiency. Use these papers to practice regularly and track your progress. Remember, consistent practice is key to mastering English Language.

Progress Tracker Tick the papers as you complete them.

- ☐ Sample Paper 1 _____ (Fill your score)
- ☐ Sample Paper 2 _____ (Fill your score)
- ☐ Sample Paper 3 _____ (Fill your score)
- ☐ Sample Paper 4 _____ (Fill your score)
- ☐ Sample Paper 5 _____ (Fill your score)
- ☐ Sample Paper 6 _____ (Fill your score)
- ☐ Sample Paper 7 _____ (Fill your score)
- ☐ Sample Paper 8 _____ (Fill your score)
- ☐ Sample Paper 9 _____ (Fill your score)
- ☐ Sample Paper 10 _____ (Fill your score)

SQP Code : **PB-1/10**	Series *i*-**Succeed 1-25/10**	Roll No.

Sample Question Paper 01

English Language 12th (Code 801)

General Instructions

1. You are allowed additional 15 minutes for only reading the question paper.
2. You must NOT start writing during reading time.
3. It has four questions in all.
4. Answer all questions.
5. You are advised to spend not more than 45 minutes on Question 1, 55 minutes on Question 2, 30 minutes on Question 3 and 50 minutes on Question 4.
6. You should begin each answer on a fresh page.
7. The intended marks for questions are given in brackets [ ].

Time : 3 Hrs.

Max. Marks : 80

Question 1.

Write a composition (in approximately 400-450 words) on any one of the following subjects. (20)

(You are reminded that you will be rewarded for orderly and coherent presentation of material, use of appropriate style and general accuracy of spelling, punctuation and grammar.)

(i) You recently visited a tourist destination. Describe how you spent your time detailing what you saw, the experiences you had on the trip and how you felt.

(ii) You were travelling in a long-distance bus in the hills and your bus broke down at night. As it could not be repaired immediately, you were forced to spend the night at a nearby mountain village. Narrate the experience.

(iii) 'The best things in life come free.' Write **for** or **against** the statement.

(iv) Express your views on the relevance of traditional media (newspapers, radio and television) over social.

(v) Give your views on 'photographs'.

(vi) Write a short story titled 'Three Lessons'.

Question 2.

(i) Outside the gates of your school, there are a few food carts. They don't observe strict hygienic standards. You have observed so many of your students go to them immediately after the school is over. This can create health problems. As headboy/headgirl, prepare a speech on 'Healthy eating practices' to be delivered in the morning assembly. You can use the following guidelines given below

Greeting or salutations and purpose - issue of following unhygienic food standards - consequences on health - importance of eating healthy - incorporate eating healthy in daily life - call to make positive changes in your diet. (15)

(ii) As the Head of the Students' Wing of the RWA of your colony, you have been given the responsibility of organising the children of your colony and undertaking the cleanliness drive in your colony on the occasion of Independence Day. Write a proposal, in about 150 words, stating the steps you would take to effectively organise this cleanliness drive. (10)

Question 3.

Answer sections **(i) (ii)** and **(iii)**.

(i) Rewrite the following sentences according to the instructions given after each of them in the brackets. (5)

(a) This fact is too evident to require proof
(Begin: This fact is so ....)

(b) As soon as he entered the room, he slipped and fell.
(Use: Hardly..................)

(c) They showed a video of 'My Fair Lady'.
(End: .... them.)

(d) Although he had high fever, he attended the meeting.
(Begin: Despite........)

(e) Raju plays both football and cricket.
(Use: .....but.....)

(ii) In the following sentences, replace the **INCORRECT** underlined words to make the sentences meaningful and grammatically correct. (Do not copy the sentence) (5)

(a) Printed <u>by</u> the poster in large, broad letters was the word 'wanted'.
(b) The Vice-President warned <u>away</u> the continuing dangers of recession.
(c) I hope this point will become clear to you <u>from</u> the course of the lectures.
(d) The effect of medicine will vary <u>on</u> one individual to another.
(e) The rain poured <u>into</u> a hole in the roof.
(f) We must refrain <u>against</u> stealing.
(g) I have always preferred teaching <u>against</u> working in an office.
(h) He jumped <u>in</u> the river to evade the enemy.
(i) The Principal brought his staff <u>around</u> to his point of view.
(j) I was carried away <u>through</u> his impressive speech.

SP-01

(iii) Fill in the blanks in the passage given below with the appropriate form of the verb given in brackets. Do not write the passage but write the verbs in correct order. (5)

An old priest ....**(1)** (tell) his congregation, "In the next sermon, I............**(2)** (preach) to you regarding the sin of lying. In order to make you ....**(3)** (understand) my teachings, I..........**(4)** (want) you all to read the Gospel, Chapter 18. The next Sunday, as he....... **(5)** (prepare) to deliver his sermon, he ....**(6)** (ask) for a show of hands. He......... **(7)** (want) to know how many of his students ....**(8)** (read) the chapter. Every hand went up.
The priest.........**(9)** (smile) and said, "The book has only 17 chapters. I........**(10)** (proceed) with my sermon now."

Question 4.

Read the passage given below and answer the questions (i), (ii) and (iii) that follow.

The Snow Goose

(1) In the late spring of 1930, Philip Rhayader came to the abandoned lighthouse at the mouth of the river Aelder on the Essex coast. He was a painter of birds and of nature, and had withdrawn from all human society. He was afflicted with a hunched back and a deformed, twisted hand.

(2) Although physical deformity often breeds hatred of humanity in people, Rhayader did not hate anyone. His heart was filled with pity and understanding. He had mastered his handicap but he could not **master** the rebuffs he suffered because of his appearance.

The thing that drove him into seclusion was his failure to find anybody who loved him as much as he loved nature and humanity.

(3) One November afternoon, three years after Rhayader had come to the Great Marsh, a child approached his lighthouse studio. In her arms, she carried a burden. She was no more than twelve, slender, dirty, nervous and timid as a bird but, beneath the dirt, as beautiful as a fairy. She was desperately frightened of the ugly man she had come to see but greater than her fear was the need of that which she carried. For, locked in her child's heart was the knowledge, picked up somewhere in the swamp-land, that this ogre who lived in the lighthouse had magic that could heal injured things.

(4) She had never seen Rhayader before and was close to fleeing in panic at the dark apparition that appeared at the studio door, drawn by her footsteps-the black head and beard, the sinister hump and the crooked hand, bent at the wrist. She stood there staring, poised like a disturbed marsh bird for instant **flight**. But, his voice was deep and kind when he spoke to her.

'What is it, child?'

(5) She stood her ground and then edged timidly forward. The thing she carried in her arms was a large white bird and it was quite **still**. There were stains of blood on its whiteness and on her dress where she had held it to her.

(6) The girl placed it in his arms. "I found it, sir. It is hurt. Is it still alive?" "Yes. Yes, I think so. Come in, child, come in." Rhayader went inside bearing the bird, which he placed upon a table, where it moved feebly.

Curiosity overcame fear. The little girl followed and found herself in a room warmed by a coal fire shining with many coloured pictures that covered the walls and was full of a strange but pleasant smell.

(7) The bird fluttered. With his good right hand, Rhayader spread one of its immense white pinions. The end was beautifully tipped with black. Rhayader looked and marvelled and said, "Child, where did you find it?"

(8) "In the marsh, sir, where fowlers had been. What - what is it, sir?"
"It is a snow goose from Canada. But, how in heaven did it come here?"

(9) The name seemed to mean nothing to the little girl. Her deep, violet eyes, shining out of the dirt on her thin face, were fixed with concern on the injured bird.
She said, "Can you heal it, sir?"
'Yes, yes,' said Rhayader. "We will try. Come, you shall help me."

(10) There were scissors and bandages and splints on a shelf, and he was marvellously deft even with the crooked hand that managed to hold things. He said, "Ah, she has been shot, poor thing. Her leg is broken and the wing tip but not badly. We will bandage the wing closer to her body; so that, she cannot move it until it has set and then make a splint for the poor leg."

(11) Her fears forgotten, the child watched, fascinated, as he worked and fixed a fine splint to the shattered leg. "A bitter reception for a visiting princess," concluded Rhayader. "We will call her the Lost Princess. And, in a few days, she will be feeling much better. See?"

(12) He reached into his pocket and produced a handful of grains. The snow goose opened its round yellow eyes and nibbled at it. The child laughed with delight.

Adapted from *Paul Gallico-The Snow Goose*

(i) (a) Find a single word from the passage that will exactly replace the underlined word or words in the following sentences. (3)

(1) In the midst of a bustling city, being away from the people is essential for maintaining mental clarity and inner peace.

(2) The argument, lacking strength or force, failed to persuade the audience.

(3) The skilled chef transformed simple dishes into culinary masterpieces.

(b) For each of the words given below, choose the correct sentence that uses the same word unchanged in spelling but with a different meaning from that it carries in the passage. (3)

(1) master (line 6)
(a) She practiced daily so that she could quickly master the art.
(b) With regular and constant practice, you can become a master craftsman.
(c) She never managed to master the Greek language.
(d) He is determined to master every aspect of the business.

(2) flight (line 18)
(a) His flight was scheduled to land in two hours.
(b) I'll try to get on the flight down to Karachi tonight.
(c) A flight crash took place when it was in air over a tall cliff.
(d) We would like to offer our apologies for the delay to your flight today.

(3) still (line 21)
(a) Silent men, like still waters, are deep and dangerous.
(b) A good reputation sits still while a bad one runs about.
(c) If you are still adamant to go, you can do so at your own risk.
(d) Some leaves were floating about on the still lake.

SP-01

(ii) Answer the following questions in your own words as briefly as possible.

(a) Why did Rhayader live alone? (2)

(b) What was the child's reaction on first seeing Rhayader? (2)

(c) What was the child's burden? (2)

(iii) Describe how Rhayader attended to the bird (Paragraphs 6 to 12) and fascinated the girl in not more than 100 words. Failure to keep within the word limit will be penalised. (8)

Answers in Topper's Style

1. (i) Last weekend, my family planned a trip to Pondicherry. It was a great relief to get away from the bitter cold, smog and pollution of Delhi for a week. Pondicherry, or Puducherry as it is commonly referred as, is one of the Union Territories of India. It is close to the Southern state of Tamil Nadu. Being an erstwhile French colony, some colonial buildings and structures exist alongside traditional and modern Indian establishments even today. A walk around the old French Quarter feels like being transported in time and place. Here, the colonial buildings with cobble stone paths are well suited for a long stroll. One might take a bicycle ride around this place which is also referred to as White Town. There are many quiet boutiques and cozy cafes to lounge about. The bakeries here serve freshly baked delicacies.

A walk around the streets and boulevards near the French Quarter is as exciting and fun-filled as a stroll at the Promenade Beach by the seaside. Here, one has a wide view of the Bay of Bengal that washes down to the shores of the gorgeous Rock Beach. The coastline of this beach is almost a kilometre long.

Here, one might see the War Memorial at one end and the Dupleix Park at the other. The Rock Beach Promenade is filled in the evening but, even then, it is peaceful as the sound of the waters on the black rocks drowns out the noise.

Pondicherry experiences a good weather for the most part. It is a tropical, wet and dry place much like the coastal areas of Tamil Nadu. The winters are warm and good for visit to several places of interest. The majority of people in Pondicherry speak Tamil. They are very outgoing and helpful. There is a small community of the French as some important French institutions such as the Consulate and the French Institute of Pondicherry still exist.

The Sri Aurobindo Ashram founded by the famous freedom fighter and philosopher Sri Aurobindo is located on Rue de la Marine. A number of other heritage buildings and monuments may be found near Promenade Beach.

One of the most beautiful sites I visited was the Paradise Beach. It is a beach that lives up to its name. It is clean and gorgeous, and a perfect location to unwind. One feels greatly rejuvenated here as it is the perfect escape from the busy city life. The boat ride to reach this place is an experience in itself. As one reaches here, the vast shoreline gives the perfect opportunity for relaxation or a dip in the frothy waves. I think everyone should visit the place atleast once.

(ii) In this cut throat and manipulative modern world, I had believed that hospitality was a lost virtue. But I found it, unexpectedly, in a remote village on a dark and scary night. I would not call myself an inhospitable person but I would not have invited some strangers to live in my house, especially at night. I still remember the dark night that was brightened by the compassion those villagers had shown us.

This incident occurred in those days when people did not travel at night in the hilly areas of Uttarakhand and there were no mobile phones. I was going on a pilgrimage to the four Dhams- Gangotri, Yamunotri, Kedarnath and Badrinath from Rishikesh. People from different cities and different walks of life had assembled to board a bus that would take them on the journey. On our way to Yamunotri, the bus had fared pretty well but, as we were moving towards Gangotri, the bus started having problems. First, it had a flat tyre and then its engine broke down just after we had passed Rudraprayag. The night was setting in and there was no prospect of the bus being repaired right then. The conductor was worried as the region was known to be the hunting ground of many wild animals and, thus, requested us to spend the night in the village just above the road.

We were very few passengers so all of us climbed the hill to reach the village. As the village was not electrified, we could see some homes with lanterns. When we explained our plight to the villagers, they offered us a place in their houses and even provided some food and a welcome cup of tea. Further, they even arranged for us to spend the night, with the passengers being spread out among the various families inhabiting the village.

Even the next morning, they not only provided us with tea and snacks but also offered us a healthy breakfast. They even entertained us by telling us about different temples and areas that we must consider visiting on our journey. Soon, our bus from Rudraprayag arrived at the village. Before we could board the bus, they insisted on doing a small pooja for our safe journey. Then, they fared us well with a lot of homemade snacks and lunch. The warmth of those villagers transformed a misfortunate night into an experience that I will cherish till the end of my days.

(iii) **For the Motion**

Often, we observe that most people believe that for having the best things in life, you need to spend money while others say that having the best things in life does not require money. I believe that the answer to this question depends on how people define the best things. I personally believe that the best things people can have in this world are knowledge and family, both of which are free of cost.

The foremost reason why I support this idea lies in the fact that knowledge is power. What can be better than having power in this world? There are several main sources of knowledge besides our educational institutions. These include books, magazines and newspapers, certain broadcast channels (both Radio and TV) and, of course, the internet. A person can have access to all of them for free or at a nominal cost. If you get a membership of your local public library, which is usually free of cost, you can have access to an open source of information. Therefore, a person can acquire power for free by making use of these facilities provided to us in the modern world.

One of the best things in life is our family. Having supportive members who care for us and our needs is all we expect from our family. When you want to do some important work, you need people to support you, no matter what happens. When you are in difficulty, it is the family that is the first to provide help. Normally, family members are willing to go to any lengths to help one another. I will give you an instance of something that occurred last year to support my contention. We live in a joint family consisting of three generations, with everyone living together in a big house. I had fallen seriously ill due to food poisoning. I had to be admitted to a private hospital for three days. It was a reputable hospital and, hence, the charges were very high. My parents could not afford them on their own.

However, my grandfather contributed most of his one month's pension, my uncle, who lives with us, gave half his monthly salary and even my aunt contributed her bank fixed deposit amount. All of them would never dream of asking us to pay back what they had contributed. Thus, if I did not have my family's support, my parents would be put to great hardship. On this basis, I can say with conviction that knowledge and family, both of which are the best things in life, come free.

Against the Motion

I definitely think the best things in life do not come free. There are many examples I can mention to prove my statement. First of all, for anything you want in life, you have to work hard.

Nothing is given to anyone for free. For instance, if your workplace is twenty kilometres away from where you live, you will have a number of difficulties in reaching your workplace, especially due to the poor condition of public transport in your city. So, you will have to work hard to save money and buy a car, motorcycle or scooter. This is an actual fact in a real situation.

Another good example of the best things in life is a decent home where you can live peacefully with your family. Definitely, a decent home does not come free unless you are a very lucky person who has inherited one. To have a nice roof over your head, a lot of money is required. Renting a house, although temporarily cheaper, is fraught with many compromises and difficulties. The number and sizes of the rooms may not suit your lifestyle, the locality may not be as decent as you would like or the owner may have compromised on the materials used to construct it. Moreover, if you want to construct or buy a house which suits you, it will require a large sum of money which can only be obtained by doing a lot of hard work so as to save enough to possess such a house. In addition, a person who has worked hard enough to become a house owner can definitely be proud that he/she has earned it. He/she will feel that he/she has been successful in life. Moreover, raising a family is definitely not free. The routine costs of managing a family are very well-known to all parents. Children have a number of essential needs such as food, clothing, education and other essentials, all of which costs money.

Another good thing in life that is not free is your health. If you get sick, you will need to buy some medicines, or even consult a doctor. In some cases, you may need to get admitted into a hospital too. None of these come free, by any stretch of the imagination. In fact, sometimes they may prove very costly.

On the basis of all these facts, we can conclude that the best things in life do not come free.

(iv) The question over the relevance of traditional media compared to digital/social media is an often discussed topic. While social media has revolutionised the way we consume news, traditional news still holds a significant place in our news consumption.

Traditional media such as newspapers, radio and television has long been a foundational pillar of information circulation and entertainment. However, in the digital age dominated by social media platforms, their relevance is often questioned. Despite the rapid rise of social media, traditional media continues to hold significant relevance and advantages.

One key advantage of traditional media is its credibility and reliability. Established newspapers and reputable news channels have a long-standing history of adhering to journalistic standards, fact-checking and providing verified information. This credibility is crucial in an era when misinformation and fake news spread quickly on social media platforms. People often turn to traditional media for accurate and trustworthy reporting on important events and issues.

Furthermore, traditional media outlets often have the resources to conduct in-depth investigative journalism. Investigative reporting requires time, effort and financial investment which many social media platforms may not prioritise. This type of journalism plays a critical role in uncovering corruption, holding governments and corporations accountable and revealing issues that may not receive adequate attention in social media's fast-paced environment.

Another strength of traditional media is its ability to reach diverse audiences. While social media allows for targeted advertising and niche communities, traditional media still reaches large segments of the population simultaneously. Television, for example, remains a primary source of news and entertainment for millions of households worldwide. Radio continues to be a preferred medium for commuting and local news updates while newspapers offer in-depth analysis and perspectives that are often lacking in social media's short-form content.

Additionally, traditional media provides a curated experience. Editors and journalists curate stories and prioritise news based on their relevance and impact helping audiences navigate through the vast amount of information available. This editorial oversight is valuable in guiding public discourse and shaping societal opinions on important issues.

Despite these strengths, traditional media faces challenges in competing with the immediacy and interactivity of social media. Social media platforms allow for real-time updates, user-generated content and instant feedback from audiences. They facilitate greater engagement and interaction enabling individuals to participate in discussions and share their own perspectives widely.

Moreover, social media's algorithms cater content to individual preferences creating echo chambers where users may only see information that aligns with their existing beliefs. This phenomenon challenges the diversity of viewpoints that traditional media strives to provide.

In conclusion, while social media has revolutionised how information is shared and consumed, traditional media remains relevant and essential in today's media landscape. Its credibility, investigative capabilities, broad reach and curated experience continue to serve as important pillars of democracy and public discourse. The symbiotic relationship between traditional media and social media offers opportunities for both to complement each other's strengths and mitigate their respective weaknesses ensuring a balanced and informed media ecosystem for the benefit of society.

(v) **Photographs**

Everybody knows that a photograph or picture is worth a thousand words but a photograph is worth a thousand memories too.

Photographs help us remember the past as well as the people who were a part of our past. They preserve our memories of past, memories that are important to us. The memories that could be otherwise easily forgotten are kept fresh in our minds through photographs. A photograph brings back memories of the day it was taken, the people who were there and even the events that occurred that day when someone stood behind a camera, asked us to smile or say 'Cheese' and pressed the shutter button.

I have a number of family photographs in which I can also be seen, right from the age of four. Other photographs of the family in which I cannot be seen have not been discarded for they hold relevance to a loved one. I can look at each one and tell people what was happening when it was taken, where I was, who I was with and why.

I have one particular photograph which I like best. I love to see it time and again. It shows me with my cousins, grandma and younger sister on the day we were leaving my grandma's house in our ancestral village to come back home. I was also bringing my grandma and two cousins along. It was the end of my summer holidays when I was studying in Class III. In that picture, my sister's hair as well as mine was in two French braids because my aunt was very good at braiding hair. That photograph brings back memories of village life as I never went back to the village again. It reminds me of the clothes I was wearing and also of my constant worry that my skirt had become too short as I was growing taller.

I regret that only one member of my family does not have a photograph taken with me. It is my grandpa.
I was only a year old when he died. Now, I'll never get a photograph with him. Nothing will trigger a flow of memories when my memory itself begins to fade away. I won't be able to look back at a photograph and say, "Here I am with my grandpa at grandma's table when he would come upstairs every morning for his daily cup of tea, to read the newspaper and to check if by any chance he had won the lottery ticket."

Thus, photographs are worth a thousand memories because one glance at a photograph can bring back memories that we have otherwise forgotten.

(vi) **Three Lessons**

Once, there was a rich man in Thailand. His name was Chulong Xi. He was a very rich man. Yet, he wanted more riches and more money. One day, while walking in his garden, he saw a strange bird in a bush. It was very small but it had very beautiful and colourful features, and its voice was also very sweet. Chulong had never seen such a bird in his life. He slowly went near the bush unseen and caught the bird. Now, the bird began to speak.

"Why have you caught me?" the bird asked. "I want to make money. I can sell you for a big amount," replied Chulong. "But, you are already rich. Why do you want more?" asked the bird. "Because, I want to become richer and richer," replied Chulong.

"But, do not dream of making money through me!" said the bird. It further added, "You cannot sell me. Nobody will buy me because, in imprisonment, I lose my beauty and my sweet voice." Then, it slowly turned into a black bird.

The beautiful features were now looking like the feathers of a crow. Chulong's hopes of making money were shattered. He said angrily, "I will kill you and I will eat your meat." "Eat me! I am so small. You will not get any meat out of me," replied the bird. Chulong could not answer. The bird then suggested, "Well, set me free. In return, I shall teach you three simple but useful rules." "What is the use of the rules? I want only money," said Chulong. He was irritated. "But these rules can profit you greatly," added the bird. "Profit me! Really? Then, I shall set you free. But, how can I trust you? You may fly away," said Chulong. "I give you my word and I always keep my word," said the bird.

Chulong wanted to take the chance. He released the bird. It flew up at once. Then, it sat on the branch of a tree. Its colour started changing. It became beautiful again. Chulong asked, "Now, teach me the rules." "Certainly," said the bird.

Then, it added, "The first rule is 'Never believe everything others say'. The second rule is 'Never be sad about something you do not have'. The third rule is 'Never throw away what you have in your hand'."

"You silly bird," shouted Chulong. He added, "These three rules are known to everyone. You have cheated me."

But, the bird said, "Chulong, just sit down for a while. Think about all your actions of today. You had me in your hands but you threw me away (released me). You believed all that I said and you are sad about not having me. The rules are simple but you never followed them. Now, do you see the value of the rules?" so saying, the bird flew away and disappeared from his sight.

2. (i) Ann Wigmore, a holistic health practitioner, once said - "The food you eat can either be the safest and most powerful form of medicine or the slowest form of poison."

Good morning respected teachers and dear peers. Today, standing before you as your head boy/girl, I am deeply concerned about the eating practices prevalent amongst us all. The statement I just quoted means that the food we choose to eat either makes us healthy or affects us adversely. Therefore, we must make wise choices.

Every one of us has stopped at the food carts stationed outside our school gates. They attract us with their tempting offerings yet their adherence to hygienic standards remains questionable at best. Despite this, we gather to the carts without a second thought, oblivious to the potential consequences on our health.

Consuming food from unhygienic sources poses a wide range of health risks, from food borne illnesses to serious infections. While the instant gratification of indulging in these treats may be enticing, the long term effects on our health is anything but desirable. These health problems do not end with just you falling sick, they lead to a series of other unfavourable consequences. They hamper your day to day lives and studies resulting in falling grades.

Eating healthy is not only nourishing for our body and minds but also includes making conscious choices that ensure our well being. It is therefore essential that we integrate healthy eating practices in our daily life. This task might appear difficult but it simply requires minor adjustments. First step should be to add whole foods to our diet. Foods such as grains, proteins, vibrant fruits and vegetables are a rich source of nutrients that not only strengthen our bodies but are also a delight for our taste buds. Additionally, we must elevate our water intake. Hydration is key to a good health and there is simply no substitute to it. Lastly, we must strive for balance in our dietary practice. While there is no harm in occasional indulgences, they must be kept at a minimum to ensure the overall wellness.

The power to make a positive change in our diet is within us. By encompassing mindfulness in our food choices and decreasing our consumption habits, we can safeguard our health and the health of those close to us. Therefore, I urge you to embrace the habit of eating healthy and also encourage your peers to do the same. Whenever you see a hawker not observing hygienic standards, create awareness about the harmful consequences of eating at such places. Let us all opt for nourishment over indulgence and prioritise quality eating. Together let's embark on a journey towards a healthier and happier future, one mindful bite at a time.

Thank you for your unwavering attention.

(ii) **Proposal for Setting Up a Cleanliness Drive**

Heading To set up a Cleanliness Drive on the occasion of Independence Day to teach the importance of cleanliness in the surroundings.

Objectives The Cleanliness Drive would promote the values of cleanliness, discipline and respect for the environment, and educate and sensitise people about the importance of cleanliness for a healthy, socially responsible, economically dynamic and progressive nation.

List of Measures

- Everyone, especially children, will be given the task to make the colony neat and clean. Brooms and separate bins for dry waste, wet waste and recyclable waste will be arranged.

- Charts and banners for painting motivational quotes informing residents about the importance of a better and clean environment will be prepared.
- Flyers will be distributed among the people of the locality and the necessity of clean surroundings will be explained to them, and they will be made aware of damage caused by plastic materials and other waste.
- Refreshments will be arranged for the children.

I hope that the proposal will be accepted so that the Cleanliness Drive can be organised well.

3. (i) (a) This fact is so evident that it does not require proof.

(b) Hardly had he entered the room when he slipped and fell.

(c) A video of 'My fair Lady' was shown by them.

(d) Despite having high fever, he attended the meeting.

(e) Not only does Raju play cricket but he also plays football.

(ii) (a) on (b) against (c) during

(d) from (e) through (f) from

(g) to (h) into (i) round

(j) by

(iii) 1. Told 2. will preach 3. understand

4. want 5. prepared 6. asked

7. wanted 8. had read 9. smiled

10. will proceed

4. (i) (a) (1) seclusion (2) feebly (3) deft

(b) (1) (b) With regular and constant practice, you can become a master craftsman.

(2) (c) A flight crash took place when it was in air over a tall cliff.

(3) (c) If you are still adamant to go, you can do so at your own risk.

(ii) (a) Rhayader lived alone as he was afflicted with a hunched back and a deformed, twisted hand. Because of his ugly physicality, he had withdrawn from all human society.

(b) The child's reaction on first seeing Rhayader was of fear. She turned panicky at his black head and beard, the sinister hump and crooked hand. She had never seen such a dark apparition-like person before.

(c) The child's burden was an injured snow goose in her hands. She came to Rhayader to seek relief and dressing for the bird.

(iii) The girl had fearfully brought an injured bird to Rhayader. While caring for the injured bird earnestly, Rhayader tried to remove the fear from the girl too. He engaged her in a conversation while skilfully spreading the birds wings to treat it. He asked her where she had found the bird and also told her about the bird's injuries. All this while, he was working on the bird. Rhayader's conversation and the manner in which he held things fascinated the girl. She, most curiously, saw how sensitively Rhayader had splinted the bird's legs and fed her some grains.

SQP Code : **PB-2/10** | Series ***i*-Succeed 2-25/10** | Roll No. | | | | | | | | |

Sample Question Paper 02

English Language 12th (Code 801)

General Instructions

1. You are allowed additional 15 minutes for only reading the question paper.
2. You must NOT start writing during reading time.
3. It has four questions in all.
4. Answer all questions.
5. You are advised to spend not more than 45 minutes on Question 1, 55 minutes on Question 2, 30 minutes on Question 3 and 50 minutes on Question 4.
6. You should begin each answer on a fresh page.
7. The intended marks for questions are given in brackets [ ].

Time : 3 Hrs.

Max. Marks : 80

Question 1.

Write a composition (in approximately 400-450 words) on any one of the following subjects. (20)

(You are reminded that you will be rewarded for orderly and coherent presentation of material, use of appropriate style and general accuracy of spelling, punctuation and grammar.)

(i) Describe the 'Career' you have decided to pursue and the factors that have influenced you to make that decision.

(ii) Narrate an incident when you travelled by an overcrowded bus.

(iii) "The policy of reservation of seats for admission to the professional courses is good for the deprived sections of society." Write **for** or **against** the motion.

(iv) Hobbies

(v) "Take care of small things and the big things will fall into place."

(vi) Write an original short story that begins with the words. "It wasn't going to be easy she knew but, somehow, she had to face him. She took a deep breath and walked into the room."

Question 2.

(i) Recently, during the State Health Minister's visit to the local civil hospital, you accompanied him as a reporter. Imagine all possible details and write a report on the visit to be published in the newspaper. (15)

(ii) As the member of the Student Council of your school, you have been asked by the Principal of your school to submit a proposal, in about 150 words, on establishing an Olympiad club to help the students who wish to appear in the International Science Olympiads. (10)

Question 3.

Answer sections **(i)**, **(ii)** and **(iii)**

(i) Rewrite the following sentences according to the instructions given after each of them in the brackets. (5)

(a) He's the funniest man I've ever met.

(Begin: I've ....)

(b) Tarmac and cement were used to build the road to Jaipur.

(Begin: They ....)

(c) As Meera did not know what to do, she kept silent.

(Begin: Not ....)

(d) She works diligently.

(Begin: How ....)

(e) She did not realise that her lies would have such a terrible consequence.

(Begin: Little did she know ....)

(ii) In the following sentences, replace the **INCORRECT** underlined words to make the sentences meaningful and grammatically correct. (Do not copy the sentence) (5)

(a) Sobha asked <u>around</u> the directions to the shop but no one seemed to know the exact address.

(b) Our car broke <u>over</u> in the middle of nowhere.

(c) Lisa broke <u>out</u> when she got to hear the results.

(d) The painting <u>up</u> the fireplace was admired by all.

(e) It seems Sam's house was broken <u>in</u> last evening.

(f) A mini riot broke <u>through</u> as soon as the ice-cream truck arrived.

(g) The opposition party worked for over a year to bring <u>down</u> the changes.

(h) The moment I bring <u>after</u> the topic of my vacation, my boss changes the topic.

(i) We haven't met in ages; let's catch <u>on</u> sometime soon.

(j) I called the team <u>up</u> to my place to celebrate.

(iii) Fill in the blanks in the passage given below with the appropriate form of the verb given in brackets. Do not write the passage but write the verb in correct order. (5)

The Banerjees, ... **(1)** (go) away leaving behind a watchman who .... **(2)** (be) partially deaf. Empty houses always had strong fascination for J. He felt that anything might .... **(3)** (happen) in them. And, even if it .... **(4)** (do not), one could ...... **(5)** (pretend) that they were the enemy's castles or even desert islands or pirate ships. In any case, there was little danger on this occasion of the fun being spoilt by others, as it so often was, because Mrs. Banerjee .... **(6)** (give) all her servants, except one, a weeks's holiday and that one spent most of his time ...... **(7)** (doze) in a chair in the kitchen. As he .... **(8)** (walk) along the road, his thoughts ...... **(9)** (go) to Shayoni, his younger sister, whom he .... **(10)** (left) at home in a state of extreme nervous tension.

SP-02

Question 4.

Read the passage given below and answer the questions (i), (ii) and (iii) that follow.

(1) My father and I left the hall and made our way out to walk across to headquarters. There were street lights round the **square** but underfoot the cobblestoned ground was dark and lumpy. My father tripped on the uneven surface and went down on one knee, trying not to fall entirely.

(2) At exactly the same moment, there was a loud bang and a sharp ringing sound and a sound of glass breaking.

(3) I bent over my father and saw that his eyes were stretched wide and his mouth grim with pain.

(4) "Run", he said, "Run for cover. For God's sake, Ben! That was a gunshot!"

(5) We were halfway across the square, easy immobile targets. He struggled to get to his feet and told me again to run and, for once, I disobeyed him.

(6) "Stay down", I told him.

(7) "You don't understand…" His voice was anguished.

(8) "Are you bleeding?"

(9) "What? I don't think so. I twisted my ankle."

(10) People ran out of the hotel drawn by the bang that re-echoed around the square. There was confusion and people were saying, "What happened, what happened?" and hands stretching down to my father to help him up. When he was well surrounded, he finally took my arm. Putting his left foot down caused him much discomfort.

(11) "That noise… " a woman said.

(12) Heads nodded, "It sounded like… Was it… a gun?"

(13) "But where? There's no one here with a gun."

(14) Everyone looked round but it was far too late to see the rifle, let alone the person shooting. My father put his arm round my shoulders for support and indicated that we should set off.

(15) We walked in a procession to the headquarters and my father called the police.

(16) I went to the open door looking across the square to the hotel.

(17) I remembered the sound of the bullet. If the bullet had been aimed at my father, and if he'd stumbled at the exact **second** that the trigger was squeezed, and if the bullet had smashed some glass so that I heard the tinkle, then why was every pane of the window in the headquarters intact?

(18) I told myself that the whole thing had been a coincidence and turned to go back inside, and saw for an instant a flash of light on broken glass down on the ground.

(19) It was a window of the shop next door that had been hit.

(20) Zing. Ricochet. Smash. The straight line could have been deflected by the curve of a cobblestone.

(21) The police arrived at the headquarters, and it was nearly two o'clock when I finally closed and bolted the doors, and switched off the lights.

(22) My father moved himself into one of the single beds in the bedroom. I lay on the second, not at all sleepy.

(23) My father said, "Ben, why didn't you run?"

(24) I answered, "I didn't want you to get shot."

(25) "So, you stood in the way..."

(26) After a while, I said, "I'd say it was a 22 rifle with a high-velocity bullet. Hitting you in the body, it quite likely won't kill you. You need to hit the **head** or the neck to be lethal. All I did was shield your head."

(27) There was a silence. Then, he said, "I'd forgotten you could shoot."

(28) "I was in the school team. We were taught by one of the country's best marksmen." I smiled in the dark. "You paid for it, you know." (***Adapted from** Penalty by Dick Francis*)

(i) (a) Find a single word from the passage that will exactly replace the underlined word or words in the sentence. (3)

(1) She has never <u>deviated</u> from her goal

(2) Her laughter's <u>repeating sound</u> in the empty halls felt like a joyful melody.

(3) Rahul was shocked to know that his friend had been diagnosed with a <u>deadly</u> disease at a young age of 28.

(b) For each of the words given below, choose the correct sentence that uses the same word unchanged in spelling but with a different meaning from that it carries in the passage. (3)

(1) square (line 2)

(a) There are numerous people in the square.
(b) The railway tube goes under the Tiananmen Square.
(c) He has a firm square jaw, shining eyes and a pointed nose.
(d) There is a massive monument in the square.

(2) second (line 27)

(a) They have a second home in Mumbai where they go during holidays.
(b) Each second in history is a fleeting time, precious and unique.
(c) She pondered for a second before answering the question.
(d) The dinner party conversation faltered for a second.

(3) head (line 43)

(a) Better be the head of a dog than the tail of a lion.
(b) Better an empty purse than an empty head.
(c) Cover your head by day as much as you will, by night as much as you can.
(d) It is the duty of the head to listen to the workers' grievances.

(ii) Answer the following questions in your own words as briefly as possible.

(a) What two things happened simultaneously when Ben and his father were walking to the headquarters? (2)

(b) What did Ben see when he looked at his father on the ground? (2)

(c) Why did Ben's father tell him to run and why did Ben disobey him? (2)

(iii) Describe the incident of the shooting in not more than 100 words (Paragraphs 1 to 10). Failure to keep within the word limit will be penalised. (8)

Answers in Topper's Style

1. (i) Career selection is very crucial in anybody's life. The type of career and course a student chooses decides his/her future and achievements in life. While choosing a career, a few things should be kept in mind. One must have an aptitude for the subject, should be focused about his/her career in that particular field and should want to be successful in that career. From the very beginning, I wanted to do something which was not very common in those days. For me, it was to become a Freelance Photographer. I was very interested in clicking photographs right from my childhood. About a century ago, when photography was invented, only simple Box-Cameras were available to take black and white photographs.

Photographic technique and equipment has come a long way since then. Exploding flash guns have progressed to compact electronic flash unit, box cameras to sophisticated computerised reflex cameras, stills to movies and part time dabblers to highly paid professionals. I thought of this career for two reasons. By being a freelancer, I could finish work according to my time or speed. There would be no targets from a company to finish the work before a set deadline. Second reason for choosing this profession is my fascination of clicking photographs during any event or of natural surroundings.

'A picture is worth a thousand words.' It describes a scene much better than words can depict. Another reason is that, in almost every sphere of human activity now-a-days, photography has come to play a very significant role.

In terms of money too, this profession has become quite lucrative. Modern professional or freelance photographers get decent pay packages and survive well from the earnings by this profession. Moreover, newspaper and magazines would never be what they are today without photography. Photographs enliven these dailies and periodicals with pictures of people and places.

Modern printing processes make an extensive use of photographic techniques. Offset printing and photocopying are examples of what photography is doing for us. All the books and magazines are now made through photographic processes. In the field of medicine too, photography is extensively used. It is also employed in Meteorology.

Moreover, as a freelance photographer, I can enjoy this profession as I can spend days at one place or travel from one place to another to photograph an event. I will have the liberty to choose time, place and location.

(ii) It was a Sunday morning and I had nothing important to do. So, I decided to visit my friend, Ajay who lives in Noida. I called him up and confirmed to go out to Gurugram to explore the Trampoline Park. We decided to meet at Connaught Place from where we would take the metro. Connaught Place is quite far from my residence in Ashok Vihar and the autorickshaw would have charged a huge amount. Going from the metro was also not an option because the metro line was undergoing repair for a week. So, I decided to board a DTC bus.

As I reached the bus stop, I saw a huge crowd on the road. They all made a dash when they saw the bus they had wanted to board coming. I had to wait for about 15 minutes before I saw the bus I had to board come to the bus stop. The sight of the bus scared me as it was packed to capacity with some passengers even hanging on to the gate. The lucky ones managed to put their toes on the foothold and left everything else to God. There is no need of pushing ourselves inside as it is done with full force by those who board the bus after us.

As I boarded the bus, the fellow commuters pushed me in. There were only 50 seats in the bus but more than hundred persons were travelling in it. The number of passengers standing was in no way less than those occupying the seats. There were eight seats reserved for the ladies but they were occupied by young men. The old women were standing and requesting the boys to vacate the seats. It was not easy to get to the exit door. One had to do some tight rope-walking as if it were a circus show.

My stop was approaching and I started pushing my way towards the door. Suddenly, I felt someone touching my purse. I tried to grab him but he had already slipped. I looked around foolishly because not only the money but also the ticket was in the same purse.

I shouted loudly and called on the driver to take the bus to the police station. He kept on driving till my stop came. He told me that I would not gain anything because the pickpocket might have got down from the bus immediately. I had learnt a new lesson of life by boarding an overcrowded DTC bus.

(iii) **For the Motion**

We all are aware that the Indian society still remains a caste–based hierarchical system. The lower caste people have remained exploited by those of the high caste and have suffered the demerits of socio-economic underdevelopment. Even the most basic of facilities that had been granted to them is still unachievable for them. In this light, reservation was created by the Constitution makers to ensure equal opportunities for them as well. Reservation since then has permeated all areas, be it education, politics and even jobs.

The aim of reservations in admission, then, to the professional courses is to bring them at par with other sections of society. Though it appears as a violation of the principle of equality, its justification is sustained by the obligation of a social welfare state. If we look at the condition of these deprived sections, we will find that most of them still live in poverty. Lack of education allows this poverty to flourish in perpetuity as children do not get properly educated and thus lack the important skills to be employed.

Article 46 of the Indian Constitution provides that the state shall promote, with special care, the educational and economic interests of the weaker sections of the people. Further, the first Constitutional Amendment Act of 1951 provides that nothing shall prevent the state from making any special provision for the advancement of any socially and educationally backward class of citizens. We must remember that a country cannot progress unless all the sections contribute together. Thus, the weaker and marginalised must raise themselves from the pits of inequality.

The Constitution was designed to help every section of society and, thus, the policy of reservation is justified. Considering that, even today, these sections face a similar state, the continuation of the reservation policy is essential.

Against the Motion

The policy of reservation stated in the Indian Constitution was designed as an ad-hoc policy for ten years but it is continually getting extensions after the end of every decade. These extensions are creating frustrations among people as some of them are deprived of opportunities to take admission in professional courses even after scoring a good and deserving percentage.

Additionally, the policy of reservation is contrary to the principle of equality which presupposes equal treatment to all and equal protection of all people. But, policies providing special privileges and extra protection to certain classes of people violates it. It violates the very spirit of democracy and does great injustice to the deserving.

Further, the reservation policy has become the main reason for brain drain and the communal disturbance taking place in the society. Due to brain drain, people are fostering resentment towards the education system. Those who are actually scoring good marks and have good references do not get the opportunity while some are getting opportunities even with very low marks. Those who suffer feel that the inequality is increasing. As a result, the need of the hour is for the institutions to focus on merit rather than caste, class or gender.

Today, very highly respected positions are occupied by undeserving candidates while the truly deserving candidates are left to struggle. Thus, not only is this policy pushing the morale of the youth downwards but also hindering the efficient growth and development of the nation.

(iv) "All work and no play makes Jack a dull boy."

Hobbies hold a very important and special place in our lives. They make our lives passionate, interesting and worth living. A hobby is a regular activity that is done for enjoyment, typically during one's leisure time. Hobbies can include anything from sports, collecting antiques, stamps or any creative artistic activity to pursuing other activity that gives happiness to a person. Any such activity that brings joy can never be a waste of time for anyone.

Life is full of stress which can be easily reduced if we develop and pursue a hobby. In today's world, children are burdened with studies, the youth suffers from anxiety caused by study or career, the middle aged and the elderly suffer from worldly and health worries. In such a depressing scenario, a good hobby acts as a safety valve releasing the mental and emotional stress. It has a stabilising effect on life by reducing stress; thereby, making people happy.

The daily chores make life a drudgery of routine. Hobbies provide the much needed variety and 'spice' to life. It often gives one motivation and inspiration to do great things. Some people have become millionaires just by collecting rare stamps and antiques. There are others who have made hobbies their profession later in life.

Hobbies can be of any type depending on one's interest and liking. Some take to collecting stamps (philately) or antiques while others pursue photography, gardening, reading, painting, writing, music, rearing animals or even sporting activities like hunting, boating, fishing, etc.

The underlying principle of any hobby is that it should be enjoyable to the person concerned. Besides enjoyment, one acquires knowledge and awareness of things which normally one would not notice. It is an ideal way to spend the leisure time in a far better way than sleeping or gossiping which is essentially a criminal waste of time.

Hobbies channel the excess time and energy of an individual towards a more productive use. This energy, if channelised in the right direction through promotion of hobbies in schools and colleges, can help the youth in becoming better citizens. Having no hobby can make one feel lost and it can make life feel extremely boring and monotonous.

Hobbies play an important part in our life and, thus, one must inculcate and nurture hobbies to enjoy its fruit throughout life. Indeed, the time spent in nurturing a hobby is time well spent.

(v) Taking care of small things is often overlooked in our fast-paced world where the focus tends to be on achieving big goals and significant milestones. However, the principle that taking care of small things leads to the smooth functioning of larger things holds great wisdom.

First, small things create the foundation upon which larger tasks and goals are built. Imagine a construction project where painstaking attention to laying each brick straight and solid ensures the stability of the entire structure. Similarly, in our daily lives, the small tasks like maintaining a tidy workspace, responding promptly to emails, or keeping appointments organised, establish the groundwork for productivity and success in bigger endeavors.

Second, paying attention to small details demonstrates a commitment to excellence. It shows that you value quality and take pride in your work, regardless of its scale. For instance, a chef who carefully selects the finest ingredients and crafts each dish is likely to earn accolades and a loyal customer base.

Moreover, addressing small matters quickly can prevent them from escalating into larger problems. In personal relationships, addressing minor misunderstandings or grievances at once can prevent resentment from festering and damaging the relationship irreparably. In business, addressing customer complaints swiftly can prevent them from escalating into larger issues that could damage the company's reputation.

Furthermore, taking care of small things cultivates discipline and good habits. Success in any endeavor often hinges on consistent effort and attention to detail. For example, a student who diligently completes daily assignments and reviews class notes is more likely to perform well on exams and achieve academic success. In contrast, neglecting these small tasks can lead to procrastination and a last-minute rush that risks good performance.

In addition, focusing on small tasks encourages mindfulness and reduces stress. Instead of being overwhelmed by the magnitude of a project or goal, breaking it down into smaller, manageable steps can make it seem less daunting. This approach allows for a clear, step-by-step progression towards the ultimate objective promoting a sense of accomplishment along the way.

In conclusion, the adage "take care of small things and the big things will fall into place" highlights the significance of attention to detail, consistency and diligence in achieving success. Whether in personal development, professional endeavours or relationships, focusing on the small tasks ensures a solid foundation for tackling larger challenges. By valuing and managing the seemingly insignificant aspects of our lives, we pave the way for greater achievements and fulfillment in the long run.

(vi) It wasn't going to be easy she knew but, somehow, she had to face him. She took a deep breath and walked into the room. She came across a dark corridor and then saw the room as the light came. He was sitting right in the front, reading a newspaper. His back was towards her. She was nervous as she knew why she was called. She also hesitated but somehow she broke the lump in her throat and called for him.

'Dad!'

He turned towards her and kept the newspaper aside. He was wearing spectacles which he suddenly removed and put on the table. His eyes were somewhat bulging out as though they were supported by a spring and could anytime come out of the socket. He asked her about her school report card. She kept looking down as she did not have the courage to see into his eyes. He waited for her response but, when there was no answer, he lost his calm and shouted angrily. He even pushed the chair violently. All the blood vanished from her face making her look completely pale.

Her father picked up the report card. As he opened it, he saw that his daughter scored all the marks in 90s. A smile came upon his angry face. His eyes turn towards his daughter who was still trembling with fear. He went towards her and hugged her. She was shocked by her father's behaviour. She felt her father's love. This was all that she had ever desired since her mother's demise.

Around two years ago, her mother expired in an accident. Her father could not accept her mother's death and grew negative towards life. He was stricter, more emotionless and more passive. He did not want his daughter to get in bad company as her mother was no more to look after her. She also got poor in studies and sometimes even failed. Two months before the boards, her father made it very clear that she must score full marks in order to get into the best college. But, when her result came, her score was 92.5% which was not enough to get her a seat in the city's best college. She was scared that her father would be disappointed. Thus, she feared revealing her marks. He, however, jumped with excitement as his daughter had worked hard and score in 90s. Now, she could enjoy her result as well as her father's love and pride.

2. (i)

Neat and Clean Hospitals

by XYZ

8th March, 20XX, Delhi: The State Health Minister visited the local civil hospital located in the Avas Vikas Colony near Pitampura on 7th March on his monthly inspection. He was pleasantly surprised to see that all of the hospital was properly maintained and found the children's ward extremely satisfactory. It was not only neat and clean but also well-maintained.

The image presented was in sharp contrast to the earlier visit to the same hospital. The dull white colour of the hospital was now covered with colourful cartoons. The things that littered the hospital were also missing and the overall atmosphere of the hospital was very positive.

The lively colours of the children's ward and the happy faces of the little children and their parents were positive indications of the situation. Everything was in order and the patients were looked after immediately and properly. Every person who was entering the hospital was getting sanitised, the door handles were also sanitised and the garbage bins were properly cleaned from time to time.

The minister was impressed by the well-maintained and hygienic atmosphere of the hospital. He appreciated the efforts of the doctors and the supporting staff of the hospital. He also advised the authorities to keep up their work by bettering the hospital and also equipping it with more and more facilities. The visit to the hospital was an eye-opener for everyone present.

(ii) **Proposal for Setting Up an Olympiad Club**

Heading To foster students' interests in Science and to help the ones who wish to appear in the International Science Olympiads, we propose to setup an Olympiad Club in our school.

Objectives An Olympiad Club will encourage the students to reach their full potential as independent learners and give their best. It will encourage more and more students to grab the opportunity of participating in Olympiads and get better results.

List of Measures

- The school library antechamber will be used for all Olympiad Club meetings and activities.
- The classes will take place thrice a week after school from 2 p.m. to 3 p.m.
- Club membership will be open for students of Classes VII to X. The club membership has been fixed at ₹ 200 per head per year.
- Some additional books on the Science subject will be provided to the club members for practice from the library.
- The club will be supervised by Mr. D. Saksena, our Science teacher.

I hope that this proposal will be accepted so that an Olympiad Club can be set up as soon as possible.

3. (i) (a) I've never met a man funnier than him.

(b) They used tarmac and cement to build the road to Jaipur.

(c) Not knowing what to do, Meera kept silent.

(d) How diligently she works!

(e) Little did she know that her lies would have such a terrible consequence.

(ii) (a) for (b) down (c) down

(d) above (e) into (f) out

(g) about (h) up (i) up

(j) over

(iii) 1. had gone 2. was 3. happen

4. did not 5. pretend 6. had given

7. dozing 8. walked 9. went

10. had left

4. (i) (a) (1) deflected (2) re-echoed (3) lethal

(b) (1) (c) He has a firm square jaw shining eyes and a pointed nose.

(2) (a) They have a second home in Mumbai where they go during holidays.

(3) (d) It is duty of the head to listen to the workers' grievances.

(ii) (a) The two things that happened simultaneously were that Ben's father tripped on the uneven surface and there was a loud bang and a sharp sound.

(b) Ben saw that his father's eyes were stretched wide and his mouth was grim with pain.

(c) Hearing the sound of gunshot, Ben's father asked him to run. Ben disobeyed his father because he did not want to leave him in danger.

(iii) At night, Ben and his father were walking towards headquarters. The ground was dark, lumpy and uneven. His father tripped on the uneven path. At the same time, there was a loud bang and the sound of glass breaking was heard. His father asked Ben to run as it was the sound of a gunshot. Ben did not run. His father who had a twisted ankle tried to get to his feet. Ben tried to help him. People came out of the hotel. There was total confusion. When Ben's father was well-surrounded by people, taking Ben's arm, he put his foot down.

SQP Code : **PB-3/10** Series ***i*-Succeed 3-25/10** Roll No. | | | | | | | | |

Sample Question Paper 03

English Language 12th (Code 801)

General Instructions

1. You are allowed additional 15 minutes for only reading the question paper.
2. You must NOT start writing during reading time.
3. It has four questions in all.
4. Answer all questions.
5. You are advised to spend not more than 45 minutes on Question 1, 55 minutes on Question 2, 30 minutes on Question 3 and 50 minutes on Question 4.
6. You should begin each answer on a fresh page.
7. The intended marks for questions are given in brackets [ ].

Time : 3 Hrs.

Max. Marks : 80

Question 1.

Write a composition (in approximately 400-450 words) on any one of the following subjects. (20)

(You are reminded that you will be rewarded for orderly and coherent presentation of material, use of appropriate style and general accuracy of spelling, punctuation and grammar.)

(i) On a train journey, you detected a bomb in the compartment and helped in evacuating and rescuing the passengers and, in the confusion, lost your baggage. Give a detailed account of your experience.

(ii) Narrate an incident that was very disappointing for you.

(iii) "Digital education can replace college education." Write **for** or **against** the motion.

(iv) Types of people

(v) Express your views on the statement "Poverty, illiteracy and unemployment are major problems faced by the country."

(vi) Write a short story beginning with the following words.
"It was a hot summer day. People were busy running around searching...."

Question 2.

(i) Write a review of the book 'Anne Frank– The Diary of the Young Girl' in about 300 words. (15)
Clues Title- author- story- background- languages

(ii) As the Head Boy/Head Girl of your school, you have been given the responsibility of organising an excursion for the students of Classes XI and XII to a Achanakmar-Amarkantak Biosphere Reserve. Write a proposal in about 150 words stating the steps you would take to successfully organise the excursion. (10)

Question 3.

Answer sections **(i)**, **(ii)** and **(iii)**

(i) Rewrite the following sentences according to the instructions given after each of them in the brackets. (5)

(a) The boss said , "What an extraordinary success!"
Begin: (The boss exclaimed..........................)

(b) Toby can buy a flat if he gets a job.
Use: (unless ....he...............)

(c) There are only a few apples left on the tree.
Begin: (There are hardly ....)

(d) It is most likely that he will pass this year.
Begin: (In all likelihood ....)

(e) Only a rich man like Mr. Baruah can live such a luxurious life.
Use: (None ....)

(ii) In the following sentences, replace the **INCORRECT** underlined words to make the sentences more meaningful and grammatically correct. (Do not copy the sentence) (5)

(a) The school board then agreed over the course to action.
(b) The benefits for providing students with lunch at school far outweigh the logical challenges.
(c) Most students benefit with interactions with fellow students outside school hours.
(d) The latest set of losses resulted by the Captain losing her job.
(e) Celine clashed from her boss in the last meeting.
(f) They clashed upon the tone of the presentation.
(g) I forgot at buy the medicine in time.
(h) I completely forgot from the strike the next day.
(i) Her speech did not touch upon various concerns of climate change.
(j) We must make this sacrifice about the benefit of the society.

(iii) Fill in the blanks in the passage given below with the appropriate form of the verb given in brackets. Do not write the passage but write the verb in correct order. (5)

As I entered the room, the first thing that .... **(1)** (strike) me as odd was the candle still ...... **(2)** (burn) on the table. The curtains had been .... **(3)** (draw) back and the room was bright. No one in their right minds...... **(4)** (keep) a candle .... **(5)** (burn) in broad daylight. The large French windows overlooked the lawn ...... **(6)** (bath) in sunlight. Marie had probably ...... **(7)** (catch) my odd stare at the table and so ...... **(8)** (move) over and blew the candle out. She then .... **(9)** (glance) at the windows and .... **(10)** (go) over to open them.

Question 4.

Read the passage given below and answer the questions (i), (ii) and (iii) that follow.

(1) Inside the cockpit of the World War II Mosquito plane, I could make out against the light of the moon, the muffled head of its pilot and the twin circles of his goggles as he looked out of the side window towards me. Carefully, he raised his right hand till I could see it in the window, fingers straight, **palm** downwards. He jabbed the fingers forward and down, meaning that we were going to descend and that I should follow him. 5

(2) I nodded and quickly brought up my own left hand so he could see it, first pointing forwards to my own control panel with one forefinger and then holding up my five spread fingers. Finally, I drew my hand across my throat. By common agreement this sign meant that I had only five minutes fuel left and then my engine would cut out. I saw the muffled, goggled, oxygen-masked head nod in understanding and then we were heading downwards towards the sheet of fog.

(3) My plane stopped trembling and plunged ahead of the Mosquito. I pulled back on the throttle, hearing the engine die to a low whistle and the other pilot was back beside me. We were diving straight towards the shrouded **land**. I glanced at my altimeter: two thousand feet, still diving.

(4) He pulled out at three hundred feet. The fog was still below us. Probably the fog bank was only from the ground to two hundred feet up, but that was more than enough to prevent a plane from landing without guidance. I could imagine the **stream** of instructions coming from the radar hut into the earphones of the man flying beside me, eighty feet away. I kept my eyes on him, following as closely as possible, afraid of losing sight for an instant, watching for his every hand-signal. Two minutes later he held up his clenched left fist in the window, then opened the fist to splay all five fingers against the glass, indicating that I should lower the undercarriage. I moved the lever downwards and felt the dull thunk as all three wheels went down, happily powered by hydraulic pressure and not dependent on the failed electrical system.

(5) The pilot of the shepherd aircraft pointed down again, for another descent. I managed to flick a glance at my fuel gauge: it was on zero, flickering feebly. For God's sake, hurry up, I prayed, for if my fuel failed me now there would be no time to climb to the minimum five hundred feet needed for bailing out. A jet fighter at one hundred feet without an engine is a death-trap with no chances for survival.

(6) For two or three minutes he seemed content to hold his position, while the sweat broke out behind my neck and began to run in streams down my back, sticking the light nylon flying suit to my skin.

(7) Quite suddenly he straightened out, so fast I almost lost him. I caught him a second later and saw his left hand flash the dive signal to me. Then he dipped towards the fog bank, I followed and we were in it, a shallow, flat descent, but a descent nevertheless and from a mere hundred feet, towards nothing. ***(Adapted from** The Shepherd by Fredrick Forsyth)*

(i) (a) Find a single word from the passage that will exactly replace the underlined word or words in the following sentences. (3)

(1) Jenna was so afraid of the gunshot that she tried to deaden the sound of her cries.

(2) During the earthquake, the windows started shaking violently.

(3) The thief kept making quick, small movements in and out of the camera sight.

(b) For each of the words given below, choose the correct sentence that uses the same word unchanged in spelling, but with a different meaning from that it carries in the passage. (3)

(1) palm (line 4)

(a) The palm tree withstood the storm very well although some of its fruits fell.
(b) My mother put some money in my palm before I left the town.
(c) Riya decided to apply henna on her left palm for her sister's wedding.
(d) My left palm has had a burning sensation since morning.

(2) land (line 14)

(a) The land next to their house is very fertile; look at the vegetables growing there.
(b) I want to buy land away from the hustle and bustle of the town.
(c) The land next to my friend's house is up for sale.
(d) If you try to land an aeroplane during a storm, the plane will crash.

(3) stream (line 18)
(a) Gorki was deep in the stream of thought when the teacher called her name.
(b) The post office received a steady stream of visitors.
(c) The stream in the valley had very little water in it.
(d) Her presentation at the conference was followed by a stream of questions.

(ii) Answer the following questions in your own words as briefly as possible.
(a) What was the first instruction of the pilot of the Mosquito plane? (2)
(b) What was the narrator's reply? (2)
(c) How did the other pilot let the narrator know that the wheels had to be lowered? (2)

(iii) Describe how the pilot of the Mosquito aircraft guided the narrator to land in not more than 100 words (Paragraphs 3 to 7). Failure to keep within the word limit will be penalised. (8)

Answers in Topper's Style

1. (i) Last year, after spending the Christmas vacations with my cousin in Jalandhar, I took a train to Lucknow. My cousins had come to see me off at the railway station. The Himgiri Express fortunately was on time. Depositing my luggage under the seat, I got down to bid farewell to them hugging and promising to meet soon.

I stretched myself on the lower berth after a long tiring day. The train was packed to capacity. Sitting opposite my berth was an old man and a child. Talking to them, I learned that they were also going to Lucknow where the old man's son was working. Soon, I settled down to sleep. While I was turning in the berth, my purse accidentally fell through the gap. I hurriedly got up to retrieve it.

While shifting the baggage of other passengers, I saw a metallic object near my purse. Sensing danger, I collected my purse and rushed to the ticket collector with the news of my discovery. Soon, there was an apprehensive crowd around my berth. The conductor and the security guard confirmed the presence of a suspicious object that could be a bomb. The frightened passengers rushed towards the door of the train to jump out. I caught hold of the alarm chain above my berth and pulled it with all my might. After what seemed like an eternity, the train came to a halt.

People trampled over each other to get out of the train with whatever luggage they could lay their hands on. I somehow managed to get out too. The compartment was soon separated from the train and people ran around searching for their dear ones.

I found Mr. Fareed Ali, the gentleman sitting opposite my berth, sobbing. He told me that his grandson was probably in the compartment and pleaded to help retrieve the child. His pleas, however, fell on deaf ears as no one was willing to enter the compartment that could blow up any moment.

Seeing the old man's grief, I decided to venture into the compartment. Taking a powerful torch, I peered in shouting, 'Salim, Salim!' My shouts were answered by a frail voice calling out for help. I saw him lying on the floor of the compartment below a berth grievously injured.

Lugging him on my shoulder, I leapt towards the door and scrambled down the train. As I set foot on the ground, the compartment blew up behind me. So strong was its impact that we were flung to the ground. The people helped us move away from the burning compartment. The old man with fell at my feet tears in his eyes thanking me for what I had done.

The relief train came at daybreak. On reaching Lucknow around noon, we were accorded a tumultuous welcome, by friends and relatives who were waiting for us since morning. As I calmed and met everyone cheerfully, I realised, I had lost my luggage.

(ii) Bacon said that travelling is a kind of education among the younger people. Hazlitt, in one of his essays, said that a journey becomes enjoyable if one hopes to get a good meal and good rest after a tiring journey and adds that travelling probably gives the maximum happiness. Perhaps, both of them have never had any experience of a journey that could have been more instructive. But I, on the other hand, am vividly aware of how disappointing a journey can be.

I had to travel to Chennai to meet my uncle and aunt for the vacations before they could leave for the UK. It was a long journey which had already dampened my mood but what I did not expect was for it to be a complete disappointment.

The journey day was indeed a day of disappointments but, being an optimist, I did not give much importance to bad omens. First of all, the taxi I hired for the station rattled noisily and emitted more smoke than an ordinary vehicle should. But, I had limited time at my disposal. So, I decided to continue my journey. After a short distance, it started sounding like an extremely tired giant and came to a sudden stop. Somehow, I reached the station in a 'tonga' (horse-cart) and found a long queue for the tickets. There were only a few minutes left for the train to leave but there was no hope of reaching the ticket window. So, I decided to travel without ticket and pay the fine during journey.

Boarding the train was itself an ordeal. Despite my healthy body, I was pushed like a shuttlecock and my luggage was mercilessly trampled upon. However, I managed to slide my way into a corner. There again, I found some persons smoking cigarettes. As I could neither stand that smell nor budge an inch, I covered my nose with my handkerchief but still felt choked.

As expected, the ticket checker came and I willingly told him about my inability to buy the ticket. He looked at me with strange eyes and all the passengers started staring at me. The ticket checker was not going to allow me to travel but I protested and told him that, if a passenger was prepared to pay the fine, he should be allowed to travel. After much argument, I convinced him and heaved a sigh of relief.

When I reached my destination, I thanked God! I thought that I would meet my uncle and aunt with a broad smile and their hospitality would make me forget the ordeals of the journey. I was dreaming of it when the rickshaw-puller was pulling the vehicle in a half- sleepy manner. To my great disappointment, I found that my uncle and aunt had gone to Shimla for a month due to some emergency and they had informed my father about it who had completely forgotten to tell me. Now, normally I would return but I did not have much money to do so. I do not want to recall this disappointing journey further because it makes me extremely sad.

(iii) **For the Motion**

In this digital age, the hunt for knowledge has gone beyond traditional books. It is not restricted to the 4 walls of a classroom. Imagine a world where the classroom is a global network, where learning happens at the pace of the student and where the credentials they earn online hold the same weightage as those of prestigious universities. This is not the future but our present reality.

Digital education allows everyone to have access to education. Traditional college education often comes with its set of restrictions be it financial or geographical. This limits opportunities for the youth. Online platforms enable one to break free of these barriers and seek education. It allows for everyone with an internet connection to get access to knowledge. Moreover, digital education provides flexibility. In a world where everyone is balancing different roles simultaneously, as well as trying to engage in different activities, the traditional education sysstem restricts them to truly engage in such.

Today, the job market is also realising the true potential of digital education and is valuing skills over any college tag. Many leading companies collaborate with leading platforms to offer specialised courses that they might want their employers to excel at. Due to the easy availability of people, employers have become specific and want people who can get the job done. They are no longer concerned with the college tag or the degree they earned.

The quality of digital education has significantly advanced in the last few years with technology taking new strides every few months. It will not be long when the CEO's of top companies will be graduates of digital education. Today, digital education stands as a robust alternative to traditional college education, ready to meet the needs of the global population.

Against the Motion

While digital education has made significant strides in accessibility and flexibility, the notion that a digital degree can fully replace a traditional college degree is fraught with challenges. Despite the conveniences and innovations offered by online learning, several critical aspects of traditional college education remain irreplaceable.

Traditional college education provides a structured learning environment that is difficult to recreate across a screen. The direct connection between the teacher and student is fundamental for facilitating discussions, debates and collaborative learning. The mentorship and networking provided by an in-person education is invaluable and can't be replaced.

The college experience in all contributes a lot towards a student's personal growth and development. Colleges are more than academic learning hubs but through their co-curriculars they foster skills in their students which are invaluable.

Even if the digital education can match up with the level of colleges, there is no way they can recreate the essence of having an in person learning experience. Skills such as networking, teamwork and leadership are important for personality development that one can only learn in traditional educational settings.

(iv) **Types of People**

There are three kinds of people in this world – the Wills, the Won'ts and the Cannots. The first accomplishes everything, the second opposes everything and the third fails in everything.

The Wills comprises of those who are so determined that they refuse to look back. Their target is all that matters and they have to achieve their goals. To them, nothing is impossible. Mahatma Gandhi was one such 'Will' and his resolute spirit and great personal courage led him to fight against all odds and lead India to independence in 1947. There are, of course, many others like him in this regard whose motivation and determination has led them to achieve everything that they have focused on.

There is another group of people called the 'Won'ts'. These contrarians oppose everyone and everything. They will neither do anything productive themselves nor will they let anyone attempt the same. It seems as though their only mission is to hamper the work of others. There are many such people in the world today who reap the dividends of others' work and will not lift a finger themselves. They find others easy to blame for their problems and create an atmosphere of negativity around themselves that negative results are the only likely outcome.

The third and final group of people is the 'Cannots'. These are the people who lack the courage and motivation to do anything. These are people who do not achieve their goals for the simple reason that they are not focused enough on their goals. Their lack of self-confidence leads them to believe that they cannot be successful and this soon turns into a self-fulfilling prophecy; they fail at almost everything they ever attempt.

While I occasionally find that I display traits that belong to either the 'Won'ts' or the 'Cannots', I identify myself with the 'Wills'. A few years ago, I was in a very bad car accident and had fractured my femur. The doctors believed that it would be difficult for me to ever walk again but, by enduring and persevering through many difficult hours of physical training, I now lead a perfectly normal life once again. I believe that my willpower definitely qualifies me among the 'Wills'.

(v) India, a country known for its cultural diversity and economic growth, faces formidable challenges in the form of poverty, illiteracy and unemployment. These issues are deeply intertwined and pose significant barriers to the nation's development and prosperity.

First poverty remains a pressing concern in India despite decades of economic progress. A large segment of the population still struggles to meet their basic needs including access to adequate food, shelter and healthcare. Poverty is often exacerbated by factors such as lack of education, limited employment opportunities and unequal distribution of wealth. Addressing poverty requires targeted interventions such as social welfare programmes, inclusive economic policies and initiatives aimed at improving access to education and healthcare.

Second, illiteracy rates in India, particularly in rural areas and among marginalised communities, contribute to the perpetuation of poverty and economic inequality. Illiteracy limits an individuals' ability to access information, gain skills, and participate fully in economic and social life. Efforts to combat illiteracy must prioritise universal access to quality education including adult literacy programmes, vocational training and initiatives that promote lifelong learning. Education not only empowers individuals but also plays a crucial role in fostering economic growth and social development.

Third unemployment remains a significant challenge, especially among the youth and in urban areas where job creation has not kept pace with population growth. High unemployment rates strain social stability and hinder inclusive economic growth. Addressing unemployment requires comprehensive strategies that promote entrepreneurship, stimulate private sector investment and enhance skill development through vocational training and education reforms.

Moreover, these challenges are exacerbated by factors such as rapid urbanisation, environmental degradation and disparities in access to resources and opportunities. Effective governance, policy coherence and collaboration among stakeholders are essential to address these complex issues holistically.

Furthermore, India's demographic dividend, with a significant proportion of its population under the age of 35, presents both opportunities and challenges. Harnessing this demographic appropriation requires investments in education, skill development and job creation to ensure productive employment and sustainable economic growth.

In conclusion, poverty, illiteracy and unemployment are critical challenges that India must address to achieve inclusive and sustainable development. By prioritising investments in education, social welfare and economic reforms, India can unlock its vast potential and create opportunities for all its citizens. Collective efforts from government, civil society and the private sector are crucial in overcoming these challenges and building a brighter future for India's diverse population.

(vi) It was a hot summer day. People were busy running around searching for cooler places to escape the scorching heat. Those who could not were stuck in their offices, or returning home, tired and withered like a dried plant. People returning home were trying to drive fast in order to reach home and be in the cool comfort of their homes. Mr. Jain was returning home after his monthly visit to the bank to collect his pension. He had waited the entire day at the bank so that he could get his pension at the earliest but he got it very late.

He had worked his entire life and now was suffering from many diseases. His illnesses took a toll on him and he went blind few years back. But, this never deterred him from his duties. He still did everything he could without the help of his pension. His wife was at home alone waiting for him. His son had worked hard at college and was now studying to be a doctor, specifically, an eye specialist. He wanted to help restore his father's sight.

People really pitied him and his helplessness. They cursed his son while the blind man's eyes welled up with tears thinking about his son. That day while returning from the bank he was lost in his thoughts, so carelessly he started crossing the busy road. Suddenly, a loud screeching of brakes was heard. Everyone rushed to see what the whole commotion was all about. Mr. Jain was lying helplessly on the road. Someone from the crowd came forward and helped him sit up.

The motorist had applied brakes at the right time and that had saved the old man. She rushed out of her car and seated the old man into her car. She apologised profusely and took him to the hospital. The doctors said that he was perfectly fine. The motorist then decided to drop the old man home. There, she saw his wife and the photo of his son. It was her best friend, Ankit. She was grateful to God that Mr. Jain was absolutely safe.

2. (i) 'Anne Frank: The Diary of a Young Girl' is a published diary of Anne Frank which was found in the attic of her hiding place during the Nazi invasion. Her father - who managed to survive the war - decided to publish it in 1947 to let the world understand not only the horrors of the Nazi rule but also the mind, intellect and wit of a young girl who was one of the victims of the war. Up until now, it has sold more than 31 million copies and has been translated into around 67 languages.

This book mainly tells about the life of an innocent young girl whose world was turned upside down out of the blue. Anne Frank was only 13 years old when the holocaust happened. Her life used to be just fine until Germany under Hitler's regime invaded Netherland. Therefore, she had to go into hiding in a cramped space she called 'The Secret Annexe'. In total, there were eight people living in that closed quarter: Anne's family and four acquaintances. Every single day, they were living in constant fear of being discovered and being sent to the Nazi's concentration camp; enslaved and persecuted.

No one could promise them safety because their life was so full of uncertainty. Living in hiding within such limited space seemed unbearable since they were restricted from doing anything. They had to bear boredom, food shortage and increased prices. They had to remain silent even when any tension and argument that occurred between them urged them to scream and shout out loud. They were forced to indulge themselves with no sound other than blazing air attacks and gunshots. The worst of all, Anne said, was that they heard the world crumbling miserably outside and they could only feel guilty for not being able to make things better. They led that life for around two years until their whereabouts were revealed to the (Gestapo German Secret State Police). Then, they were taken to the concentration camp.

Reading this book would give you a chance to live in the soul of a 13-year-old girl who had to face atrocities just because she was born a Jew. Seeing the world through the honest point of view of Anne Frank at the time of the holocaust, you will be amazed by the fact that for the girl of her age, she wasn't naive. Instead, she was really critical in responding to the events occuring around her.

Well, although it may seem monotonous at some points, her way of criticising others will not fail to entertain you and force you to turn to the next page. I really recommend this book to those who want to get a deep insights about the holocaust, social dynamics within Nazi's regime and perhaps to those who want to accompany me in feeling the heartbreak each time Anne said, "soon when everything gets normal again..." knowing that the world didn't get the chance to turn normal for Anne Frank.

(ii)

Proposal for Organsing an Excursion to
Achanakmar-Amarkantak Biosphere Reserve

Heading To foster an interest of students in wildlife and to introduce the students to the wonders of animals, life and living, we propose to organise an excursion.

Objectives The excursion to the National Park will be both enjoyable and enriching leaving some use full lessons behind with the students. The students will develop a love for the wildlife.

List of Measures

- To arrange buses for the trip.
- To make arrangements for rooms or dormitories to accommodate the students.
- To organise fun activities to keep the trip energetic and enthusiastic.
- The students will be accompanied by History and Geography teachers, Mr. Arun, Ms Asha and Ms Sumita for better understanding of wildlife.
- The trip will cost ₹ 1500 per child and will include all lodging, boarding and food charges.

I hope that this proposal will be accepted so that the excursion may be arranged as soon as possible.

3. (i) (a) The boss exclaimed that it was an extraordinary success.
(b) Unless Toby gets a job, he can't buy a flat.
(c) There are hardly any apples left on the tree.
(d) In all likelihood, he will pass this year.
(e) None but a rich man like Mr. Baruah can live such a luxurious life.

(ii) (a) of (b) of (c) from (d) in
(e) with (f) over (g) to (h) about
(i) about (j) for

(iii) 1. struck 2. burning 3. drawn 4. would keep
5. burning 6. bathed 7. caught 8. moved
9. glanced 10. went

4. (i) (a) (1) muffled (2) trembling (3) flickering
(b) (1) (a) The palm tree withstood the storm very well although some of its fruits fell.
(2) (d) If you try to land an aeroplane during a storm, the plane will crash.
(3) (c) The stream in the valley had very little water in it.

(ii) (a) The pilot of the Mosquito plane instructed the narrator to follow him as they were going to descend.
(b) The narrator nodded in agreement. With his finger gestures, he indicated that he had only five minutes worth of fuel left.
(c) The other pilot held up his clenched left fist in the window, then opened the fist to spread out all five fingers against the glass indicating that the narrator should lower the wheels.

(iii) The pilot of the Mosquito aircraft guided the narrator to land with his gestures. He first pulled at three hundred feet and instructed the narrator to lower the undercarriage which he did by using hydraulic pressure. The fuel gauge indicating zero caused nervousness for the narrator. The other pilot was satisfied with his action. When he suddenly straightened out, the narrator first got lost but followed the dive signal at once to descent to the fog bank. It was a flat descent from a mere hundred feet to the fog bank.

SQP Code : **PB-4/10** Series ***i*-Succeed 4-25/10** Roll No. | | | | | | | | |

Sample Question Paper 04

English Language 12th (Code 801)

General Instructions

1. You are allowed additional 15 minutes for only reading the question paper.
2. You must NOT start writing during reading time.
3. It has four questions in all.
4. Answer all questions.
5. You are advised to spend not more than 45 minutes on Question 1, 55 minutes on Question 2, 30 minutes on Question 3 and 50 minutes on Question 4.
6. You should begin each answer on a fresh page.
7. The intended marks for questions are given in brackets [ ].

Time : 3 Hrs.

Max. Marks : 80

Question 1.

Write a composition (in approximately 400-450 words) on any one of the following subjects. (20)

(You are reminded that you will be rewarded for orderly and coherent presentation of material, use of appropriate style and general accuracy of spelling, punctuation and grammar.)

(i) It was a long awaited climax to your period of training for the parachute regiment - the day of the first jump! Describe how you prepared yourself for the parachute drop, the drop itself and your feelings after the event.

(ii) Narrate an incident that you would aptly title as 'The Unusual Summer Vacation'.

(iii) "Films should be made to escape from reality not remind us of how grim life is." Argue **for** or **against** this statement.

(iv) Peace

(v) Express your views on 'Should punishment be retributive or reformatory?'

(vi) Write an original short story beginning with the following words. "She was delighted to find the sealed envelope lying on her table. As she reached for it ...."

Question 2.

(i) Through advertisements, commercial products are promoted by celebrities from various fields like sports, films, etc. Such advertisements have become a big business. They leave a strong influence on all, but especially on young minds.

Using the given clues, write an article on "The Impact of Advertisements on the Younger Generation". (15)

Digital Age—Idealised life style and beauty standards portrayed—Influencing consumer behaviour—shaping societal norms and values—positive and negative impact on the younger generation—stimulates critical thinking and creativity.

(ii) Write a proposal for the purchase of water purifiers for replacement of the purifiers already existent in the school in about 150 words. (10)

Question 3.

Answer sections **(i)**, **(ii)** and **(iii)**

(i) Rewrite the following sentences according to the instructions given after each of them in the brackets. (5)

(a) Candidates may not bring textbooks into the examination hall.
Begin: (Candidates are ....)

(b) He is so short that he cannot be a soldier.
Use: (......... too ....be............)

(c) The book I had read earlier was better than this book.
Use: (.........not as good..............)

(d) They said that he had broken the chair.
Begin: (They accused ....)

(e) All the girls have brought their books with them.
End: (...................... each of the girls)

(ii) In the following sentences, replace the **INCORRECT** underlined words to make the sentences more meaningful and grammatically correct. (Do not copy the sentence) (5)

(a) Do you want to take <u>on</u> every single object from the box?
(b) The plane must take <u>up</u> before it gets dark.
(c) The children spoke <u>above</u> a whisper as they were scared.
(d) We must not speak ill about a person <u>against</u> his/her back.
(e) Walking barefoot <u>above</u> the grass is very good for health.
(f) He disliked the play so much that he walked <u>away</u> in the middle of the first act.
(g) This rule doesn't apply <u>for</u> you as you are less then eighteen years old.
(h) You must apply <u>at</u> the job immediately .
(i) They have been living in Delhi <u>since</u> ten years.
(j) Mrs. Kapur has been living in Chennai <u>from</u> 2002.

(iii) Fill in the blanks in the passage given below with the appropriate form of the verb given below with the appropriate from of the verb given in brackets. Do not write the passage but write the verb in correct order. (5)

Two carpenters .... **(1)** (work) on Mr. Sharma's roof. When they ...... **(2)** (stop) work at 6 p.m., they ...... **(3)** (leave) their ladder ...... **(4)** (lean) against the house. At 7 p.m., Raju, a thief, passed by the house and ...... **(5)** (see) the ladder. The house ...... **(6)** (be) now empty as Mr. and Mrs. Sharma .... **(7)** (go) to the market. Raju .... **(8)** (climb) up the ladder, ... **(9)** (get) in through a first-floor window and .... **(10)** (go) straight to the main bedroom where he stole all of Mrs. Sharma's jewellery.

Question 4.

Read the passage given below and answer the questions (i), (ii) and (iii) that follow.

(1) At the Literary Society's meeting, Isola read out the letters written to her Granny Pheen, when she was but a little girl. They were from a very kind man - a complete stranger. Isola told us how these letters came to be written.

(2) When Granny Pheen was nine years old, her cat died. Heartbroken, sitting in the middle of the road, she was sobbing her heart out.

(3) A carriage, driving far too fast, came within a whisker of running her down. A very big man in a dark coat with a fur collar, jumped out, leaned over Pheen and asked if he could help her. Granny Pheen said she was beyond help. Muffin, her cat, was dead.

(4) The man said, 'Of course, Muffin's not dead. You do know cats have nine lives, don't you?' When Pheen said yes, the man said, 'Well, I happen to know your Muffin was only on her third life, so she has six lives left.' Pheen asked how he knew. He said he always knew - cats would often appear in his **mind** and chat with him. Well, not in words, of course, but in pictures.

(5) He sat down on the road beside her and told her to keep **still**-very still. He would see if Muffin wanted to visit him. They sat in silence for several minutes, when suddenly the man grabbed Pheen's hand.

(6) 'Ah-yes! There she is! She's being born this minute! In a mansion - in France. There's a little boy petting her, he's going to call her Solange. This Solange has great spirit, great verve - I can tell already! She is going to have a long, venturesome life'.

(7) Granny Pheen was so rapt by Muffin's new fate that she stopped crying. The man said he would visit Solange every so often and find out how she was faring.

(8) He asked for Granny Pheen's name and the name of the farm where she lived, got back into the carriage and left.

(9) Absurd as all this **sounds**, Granny Pheen did receive eight long letters, Isola then read them out. They were all about Muffin's life as the French cat - Solange. She was, apparently, something of a feline musketeer. She was no idle cat, lolling about on cushions, lapping up cream - she lived through one wild adventure after another - the only cat ever to be awarded the red rosette of the Legion of Honour.

(10) What a story this man had made up for Pheen - lively, witty, full of drama and suspense. We were enchanted, speechless at the reading. When it was over (and much applauded), I asked Isola if I could see the letters and she handed them to me.

The writer had signed his letters with a grand flourish .

Very Truly Yours,

O.F.O'F. W.W.

It was highly possible that Isola had inherited eight letters written by Oscar Wilde, for who else could have had such a preposterous name as Oscar Fingal O'Flahertie Willis Wilde.

(***Adapted from*** *The Guernsey Literary and Potato Peel Pie Society*)
By Mary Ann Shaffer and Annie Barrows

(i) (a) Find a single word from the passage that will exactly replace the underlined word or words in the following sentences. (3)

(1) After hearing about the death of her beloved pet, she was very sad.

(2) Sounds of his loud crying could be heard from another room.

(3) The judge was appalled at the ridiculous argument presented by the lawyer.

(b) For each of the words given below, choose the correct sentence that uses the same word unchanged in spelling but with a different meaning from that it carries in the passage. (3)

(1) mind (line 12)
- (a) There is no doubt in my mind that she was telling the truth.
- (b) Would you mind my smoking in your room for a while?
- (c) The smaller the mind, the greater the conceit.
- (d) Those words stayed in her mind all afternoon.

(2) still (line 14)
- (a) The moment he looked at me, I stilled.
- (b) The crowd stood still and waited for her.
- (c) The doctor told her to stay still for the procedure.
- (d) I am sorry but there is still worse news for you.

(3) sounds (line 24)
- (a) It sounds like I might be able to work something out.
- (b) The story sounds like a fairy tale to me.
- (c) Try to be familiar with different sounds and smells of the forest.
- (d) That sounds like your kind of logic - always thinking of the other person first.

(ii) Answer the following questions in your own words as briefly as possible.
- (a) Where did Isola get the letters from to read at the Literary Society's meeting? (2)
- (b) Who consoled Granny Pheen when she was heart-broken? What did he say about Muffin's lives? (2)
- (c) What did the man say when Granny Pheen asked him how he knew about cats' lives? (2)

(iii) In not more than 100 words, summarise why the eight letters were a treasure to Granny Pheen (Paragraphs 2 to 10). Failure to keep within the word limit will be penalised. (8)

Answers in Topper's Style

1. (i) 'Jump', barked the instructor, standing near the exit of the plane, as it soared 10,000 ft above sea level. My heart skipped a beat, as I nervously fidgeted my feet, trying to muster courage. After an agonising long minute, he glared furiously at me shouting, "Jump you fool, others are waiting their turn." As if on cue, I stepped aside making way for Mohan standing just behind me to go ahead and jump. Mohan looked contemptuously at me and with a grin ran towards the exit. He was off the plane in a jiffy. It all appeared so simple as I saw him jump.

It was, however, not so simple as it appeared because the para jump was the climax of a month-long training. This was a crucial exercise for the parachute regiment of the NCC battalion in school. The first week was spent familiarising the students with the basics of aero dynamics. This was followed by practical classes, where the basics of the parachutes was explained, which was followed by the technique of maneuvering the chute taking into account the direction of the wind. Such techniques help in moving away from trees and high rise buildings while landing. The training programme finally concluded with a special psychological session, to mentally prepare us for the jump. The parting advice of the instructor was - "Never look down before you jump and never to panic and lose cool while hurtling down."

Just a moment ago, I was feeling very confident. Yet, here I was, fumbling and afraid of taking the plunge. The question that bothered me - what if the chute failed to open? The very thought made my legs quiver. As I glanced down from the air plane window, the words of the instructor rang in my ears, "Never look down before you jump."

'Next', barked the instructor. I looked behind me making way but there was nobody - behind. Steeling myself, I ran toward the exit and leaped into space, with my eyes firmly shut and with a prayer on my lips. My heart literally jumped into my mouth as I hurtled down like a stone. The first few seconds were very agonising as I fumbled with the string of the parachute. I felt a sudden tug as it opened halting my speedy descent. It was smooth sailing thereafter as I drifted in and out of the clouds.

The scenic beauty from the great height was indeed breathtaking. I shouted with delight seeing the green fields, meadows and orchards in the countryside. The match box size high rise buildings, the serpentine roads and canals continued to grow in size as the parachute continued to descend. I waved out to my friends sailing in the vicinity who also seemed to be having the time of their life. Steering away from the trees, I finally landed on a small field close to our base camp. Folding my parachute, I walked up to Mohan who was waiting for me. Together, we jogged down to the camp, sharing our experience.

It was a thrilling experience that I shall never forget in my life. The thought of the traumatising seconds, just before and after the jump makes my hairs stand on end. But, then, what is life without risk and adventure? The parachute jump enhanced my willpower making me more self-confident.
It added a new facet to my personality which was hitherto unknown to me.

(ii) **The Unusual Summer Vacation**

Summer, in most parts of India, is hot and unpleasant. But, it is also the time when schools close down and we get a long vacation. Though I hate the hot weather which is invariably accompanied by flies and dust, I enjoy the variety of fruits especially the mangoes and litchees. The cool drinks that mother always keeps ready in the fridge are also very soothing.

Above all, I look forward to my father coming home on leave. Being in the navy, he is away at sea most of the time. When he comes, home, we leave for a long stay to some hill station. The cool climate, the greenery all around, the long hikes and the family being together are all things that I eagerly look forward to.

It was the summer when I was in Class VII. One morning, mother came and broke the news that father would not be able to come home that summer. He had been put on emergency duty. My sister and I felt like deflated balloons. We sighed at the thought of not going to a hill station and not meeting father until the next holidays and spending 14 months in the hot Delhi summers. On the last day of school, we dragged our feet home, not at all happy at the prospect of having to spend a boring vacation at home.

The first few days were not too bad, as we enjoyed the no-hurry, no-study schedule. The desert cooler, of course, was a great relief. Our family, being very environment conscious does not use an AC. We were chatting over cool drinks when mother waved two blue slips at us. They were the forms of the swimming pool nearby. We could start right away. What a surprise!

When we went there, we met many of our classmates. From that day, the pool became the centre of our vacations. All of us being good swimmers, the coach gave us liberty to play games. Water polo was fun as was under water 'catch'. Mother always packed some sandwiches and a fruit juice or a milkshake which we shared with our friends when we strolled back home. The days just flew by, though I missed father and our trip to the hills, summers in Delhi were not so bad after all.

(iii) **For the Motion**

How many of us wear the clothes of the opposite gender everyday just to please someone or how many of us dab on makeup and sleep to wake up as graceful as ever. Or how many of us have a talking pet or have an encounter with the extra-terrestrial creatures? None of us do, do we?

Yet, we all love watching cartoon movies, the *Jurassic Park* series and the *Harry Potter* series amongst the innumerable options of fantastical movies that are taken from the diverse genres of family drama, comedy, romance, tragedy and so on. Thus, with the view that films present what mostly cannot happen in our day-to-day lives, I concur with the statement.

Films, I believe, are merely made for entertainment and the relaxation of mind and body. While it may mimic reality and talk about how life could be or should be, it should not show the sadness and anxiety that we associate with life every day. If we had wanted to see and come face-to face with the grim reality of life, we would rather visit an old age home, an orphanage, a hospital or a slum instead of a movie theatre since they are not only free but also provide a real picture.

When we go to watch a movie anywhere, be it a movie theater or the comforts of our home, we expect to forget all the worries of our life, get rid of stress and anxieties and just enjoy the movie. In doing so, we want to listen to music, imagine the storyline, get involves in the imaginative world of movie and applaud the technicalities involved in the movie.

Storytelling, as we all know, is a powerful medium of communication, use of creative faculties and enjoyment. Be it fairy tales, or tales from the religious texts or fictional stories, storytelling has since long been the source of entertainment and fun as well as frolic for all. Now, to this mode of enjoyment, add the concept of visual and audio and see that yow you have a much more realistic version of the story happening right in front of your eyes.

Against the Motion

While I agree that movies are a huge, almost mammoth, source of entertainment for everyone, irrespective of the stratums of society, I differ in the opinion that its motive is only limited to entertainment. My opponent had just stated that storytelling as an art served to entertain but, if we look closely at the tales that were told, we will find that most of them are moral.

From morality plays that talks about human virtues and vices, to fables from the religious texts, all of the tales have had a didactic purpose, teaching about how to reduce the sadness that fills our life.

Films offer viewer with an idea that they should think upon so that they can act on it. This, in addition with the growing fan base of movies and craze of people for watching movies, makes it all the more essential for movies to represent life in all its real glory. In reality, people struggle from many personal and social issues. Be it health conditions like Aids, hair falling problem or the struggles of being a women or other gender, etc. all of these can and should be represented in movies.

In addition, our country is faced with innumerable problems, including corruption, lack of efficient law enforcement, crimes, violence, addiction, etc. We always say that we, the people of the nation, have to work towards the cause to solve the issue. But, how would we know that a problems exists and to what extent. This can be easily done with the help of movies and shows that can lead people to understand the gravity of the situation and join hands for the cause.

While I do agree that tackling heavy topics of real life may make a movie boring, it does not necessarily mean that they should altogether be avoided. Using innovative creative story writing techniques and dialogues, a serious movie can be made comical and entertaining. We all remember the movie '3 Idiots'. While the movie may have been based on a novel, it handles the strict and stringent regimen and ragging issues with such a dexterity that the movie becomes entertaining while presenting the grim reality of life.

(iv) **Peace**

Peace is a word that has significant meaning in our lives yet its true essence has never been understood. At its core, peace is not only the absence of war or violence but is also a state of harmony, tranquility and respect among humans. It has always been a collaborative effort rooted in understanding, empathy and a commitment to justice.

Peace has always been understood in the context of war. One of the key aspect for upholding peace is the resolution of conflict through dialogue and not to resort to violence and aggression. When disputes arise, whether on a personal or global level we must be open to communication. When we sit and try to have a conversation, we often find how the most complex of the problems can be resolved through talking. In today's world, people have become vicious not caring about humanity. We must collectively make strides for a peaceful world where humans are treated kindly by fellow humans. War crimes such as blatant disregard of human rights and dignity of individuals should not be encouraged.

Peace is universal as it encompasses people of all gender, race, religion or socio-economic status. It is not bound to any boundary that might restrict someone from attaining a peaceful living. In a broader aspect, a peaceful world also respects diversity. It facilitates an environment of cultural acceptance and cooperation where everyone is treated equally and no one is oppressed based on any bias.

Education plays an important role in promoting peaceful coexistence. By fostering values such as compassion, tolerance and non – violence amongst civilians, we try to cultivate a generation which is more committed to building a peaceful world. Education is the key to bridge cultural divides and prejudices.

Peace is not a passive state but an active endeavour that requires constant efforts at individual, community and global levels. It involves resolving conflicts peacefully, upholding human rights, promoting education and understanding, and fostering environmental sustainability. By embracing these principles and working collaboratively towards a shared vision of peace, we can create a world where harmony, justice and prosperity prevail for all.

(v) The debate between retributive and reformatory punishment philosophies has long been a subject of debate in discussions about justice and the penal system. Retributive punishment focuses on the idea that punishment should be proportionate to the offense committed, aiming to satisfy a sense of justice and provide closure for victims and society. On the other hand, reformatory punishment emphasises rehabilitation and aims to reform offenders through education, therapy and skills training with the goal of reintegrating them into society as productive members.

Advocates of retributive punishment argue that it upholds the principle of accountability and serves as a barrier against future crimes. By imposing punishments that fit the severity of the offense, retributive justice seeks to restore the moral balance disrupted by criminal acts. This approach is rooted in the belief that offenders deserve to suffer consequences for their actions and that society has a right to seek retribution for the harm caused.

However, critics of retributive punishment point out its potential for perpetuating cycles of violence and focusing solely on punishment rather than addressing underlying causes of criminal behaviour. They argue that disciplinary measures often fail to rehabilitate offenders or prevent relapse, leading to overcrowded prisons and strained judicial systems. Moreover, retributive justice can be seen as prioritising vengeance over restoration and healing, potentially undermining efforts to promote a more compassionate and rehabilitative approach to justice.

In contrast, reformatory punishment advocates contend that rehabilitation offers a more humane and effective approach to dealing with crime. By focusing on addressing root causes such as poverty, lack of education, mental health issues and substance abuse, reformatory justice seeks to break the cycle of criminal behavior and promote long-term societal well-being. Programmes that provide education, vocational training, counselling and support services aim to equip offenders with the skills and resources needed to lead law-abiding lives upon their release.

Nevertheless, critics of reformatory punishment argue that it may be perceived as lenient or overly forgiving, potentially undermining the deterrent effect of punishment. They raise concerns about the efficacy of rehabilitation programmes and the challenge of accurately assessing an offender's readiness for reintegration into society.

Ultimately, the ideal approach to punishment likely lies in a balanced combination of retributive and reformatory principles, tailored to the specific circumstances of each case and the needs of individuals involved. Incorporating elements of both philosophies can help achieve justice by holding offenders accountable for their actions while also offering opportunities for rehabilitation and restoration.

(vi) She was delighted to find the sealed envelope lying on her table. As she reached for it, she received a call from an unknown number. She was trying to figure out whose number it was but she couldn't recognise it. She didn't receive the call the first time as she was so excited to check the contents of that envelope but, by the time she would open it, she received a call from the same number again on her phone.

As she realised that the call might be urgent, she answered it. She wasn't aware that this call could change her life completely as she got a shocking news!

The person gave her news that her dad was martyred in a terror attack and that her family was being called to complete the further documentation. He further informed that the body of her father will be handed over to the family after that. The girl was numb and couldn't speak a word. She didn't know how to react and how to inform her mother and younger sibling. She was so excited to check her envelope that she didn't even realise that there was a breaking news on the television where this news was highlighted. But then, she was a strong girl just like her brave father. She gathered her guts and went to her mother to inform her about this news. Wiping the tears from her eyes, she called her sibling and both the sisters gave this news to their mother. Then, all three of them informed their relatives and waited for another call. After all the procedures, the last rites were carried out with all the respect that her father deserved.

The family, after all the rituals, got a call from the Chief Minister of her state for the compensation amount and a job in the government office for her mother. The girl accepted the job offer but denied the compensation amount as this amount would not bring her father back. Since the family was always inspired by their father's background, everyone was brave enough to face this situation and move on. The girls decided that they will not take anyone's favour but, with their hard work and dedication, they will make their father proud. The eldest daughter studied hard and, with all her hard work, she cleared, her exams and decided to serve the Indian Army like her father. The mother was stupefied by her daughter's decision and supported her in this as the whole family was proud of the daughter who was fulfilling her father's dream to serve the nation.

2\. (i) **The Impact of Advertisements on the Younger Generation**

by Rishabh Mehta

Advertisements wield significant influence over the younger generation, shaping their perceptions, preferences and behaviours in profound ways. In today's digital age, where advertising has invaded various media platforms, its impact on youth culture and consumerism cannot be overstated.

First, advertisements often portray idealised lifestyles, beauty standards and material possessions that can create unrealistic expectations among young people. This can lead to feelings of inadequacy or dissatisfaction with their own lives, appearance or possessions as they compare themselves to the exaggerated images and lifestyles depicted in ads. For example, cosmetic advertisements frequently promote flawless skin or perfect bodies, setting unattainable standards for many adolescents.

Second advertisements heavily influence consumer behaviour by promoting products and brands directly to young audiences. Advertisers target children and teenagers because they represent a lucrative market with significant purchasing power and influence over family spending. Through catchy jingles, trendy endorsements, and compelling visuals, ads can create strong desires and cravings for products among impressionable youth.

Moreover, advertisements can shape societal norms and values by reinforcing stereotypes or promoting certain attitudes and behaviors. Gender roles, for instance, are often reinforced through advertising, portraying girls and boys in stereotypical roles and perpetuating traditional norms. This can impact young people's perceptions of gender equality and influence their social interactions and career aspirations.

Furthermore, the rise of digital advertising and social media has intensified the impact on the younger generation. Online platforms use targeted advertising algorithms that track users' browsing history and behaviour to deliver personalised ads. This personalised marketing can further reinforce consumerist tendencies and influence purchasing decisions based on individual preferences and interests.

However, not all impacts of advertisements on young people are negative. Advertisements can also educate and inform promoting important social messages such as health awareness, environmental conservation and social responsibility. Ad campaigns advocating for causes like anti-bullying, mental health awareness and environmental sustainability can raise awareness and inspire positive changes among youth.

Additionally, advertisements can stimulate creativity and critical thinking among young people. Analysing and deconstructing advertisements can help the youth develop media literacy skills, enabling them to discern between credible information and persuasive messages. This empowers them to make informed decisions and resist manipulative marketing tactics.

In conclusion, while advertisements wield considerable influence over the younger generation, their impact is multifaceted and complex. Advertisements shape attitudes perceptions, and behaviors among youth influencing their consumer choices, societal values and self-perceptions. By promoting media literacy, fostering critical thinking skills and encouraging responsible advertising practices, society can mitigate potential negative impacts while harnessing the positive potential of advertising to educate, inspire and empower the younger generation.

(ii) **Proposal for Purchase of Water Purifiers**

Heading To improve the health of students. It will also raise the standard of school.

Objectives To prevent the spread of water borne diseases and reduce absenteeism; thus, improving the quality of education of the school.

List of Measures

- The school authorities will invite quotations from reliable vendors.
- The preferable purifiers are of LG or Kent brand.
- A budget of around 1.5 lakh will be set for 8 good quality RO purifiers.
- The already existing RO purifiers will be replaced.
- An AMC for all the purifiers will be taken from the company of the purifiers.

I hope that this proposal will be accepted so that the RO Purifiers can be setup as soon as possible.

3. (i) (a) Candidates are not allowed to bring textbooks into the examination hall.

(b) He is too short to be a soldier.

(c) This book is not as good as the one I had read earlier.

(d) They accused him of breaking the chair.

(e) The books were brought by each of the girls.

(ii) (a) away (b) off (c) in (d) behind
(e) on (f) out (g) to (h) for
(i) for (j) since

(iii) 1. were working 2. stopped 3. left 4. leaning
5. saw 6. was 7. had gone 8. climbed
9. got 10. went

4. (i) (a) (1) heartbroken (2) sobbing (3) preposterous

(b) (1) (b) Would you mind my smoking in your room for a while?
(2) (d) I am sorry but there is still worse news for you.
(3) (c) Try to be familiar with different sounds and smells of the forest.

(ii) (a) Isola got the letters from her Granny written to her by a stranger when she was but a small girl.

(b) A stranger consoled Granny Pheen when she was heart-broken. He said that Muffin was not really dead as a cat had nine lives; he added that she was on her third life.

(c) The man told Granny Pheen that he knew about cats lives as cats' would often appear in his mind and chat with him.

(iii) When Granny Pheen was nine, her cat died which made her heart-broken. At that point, a man came and consoled her saying that her cat was not dead. As a cat had nine lives; he said her cat was on her third life. She was actually being born in a mansion in France. The man said that he knew about it as cats often appeared in his mind to chat. Granny Pheen stopped crying. The man went away and wrote her long letters about the new life of her cat, named Solange. Solange had been honoured for her various adventures.

SQP Code : **PB-5/10** Series ***i*-Succeed 5-25/10** Roll No. | | | | | | | | |

Sample Question Paper 05

English Language 12th (Code 801)

General Instructions

1. You are allowed additional 15 minutes for only reading the question paper.
2. You must NOT start writing during reading time.
3. It has four questions in all.
4. Answer all questions.
5. You are advised to spend not more than 45 minutes on Question 1, 55 minutes on Question 2, 30 minutes on Question 3 and 50 minutes on Question 4.
6. You should begin each answer on a fresh page.
7. The intended marks for questions are given in brackets [ ].

Time : 3 Hrs.

Max. Marks : 80

Question 1.

Write a composition (in approximately 400-450 words) on any one of the following subjects. (20)

(You are reminded that you will be rewarded for orderly and coherent presentation of material, use of appropriate style and general accuracy of spelling, punctuation and grammar.)

(i) Describe the scene at a busy railway station during the holiday season. Your description should recall vividly the bustle and confusion of such a scene.

(ii) You have been living in your ancestral house since your birth. The house has been given to the government by your father because the Delhi Metro line has to pass from there. Narrate the incidence of how they broke the news to you and describe your feelings about moving out of this house.

(iii) "The only way to minimise human suffering and pain is to control our needs." Write **for** or **against** the topic.

(iv) Memories

(v) Express your views on 'Films are the mirror of Society'.

(vi) Write an original short story entitled 'The Gift'.

Question 2.

(i) You have noticed that there has been a surge in road accidents amongst students. As Principal, prepare a speech on 'Safe Driving' to be delivered in the morning assembly. Write a speech following the guidelines given below. (15)

Greeting or salutations and purpose- importance of driving safely and keys issues such as cause of road accidents- understanding traffic rules and regulations- creating awareness and education- role of safe driving practices- need of the hour.

(ii) As the President of the Social Service Club of your school, you want to arrange a visit to an orphanage and spend a day with the residents. Write a proposal in not more than 150 words stating the steps you would take to successfully brighten their day. (10)

Question 3.

Answer sections **(i)**, **(ii)** and **(iii)**

(i) Rewrite the following sentences according to the instructions given after each of them in the brackets. (5)

(a) The tenure of my stay is doubtful.
Use: (How..................)

(b) She was too full to have another meal.
Begin: (She was so...................)

(c) Ranjeet said, "Sheela, Why don't you take the advice of your parents in this matter?"
Begin: (Ranjeet asked Sheela ....)

(d) Rahul has not been to school for over two months.
Use: It.........since........)

(e) I lost the book.
End: (.............by me.)

(ii) In the following sentences, replace the **INCORRECT** underlined words to make the sentences meaningful and grammatical correct. (Do not copy the sentence) (5)

(a) We failed to agree <u>to</u> a common plan of action.
(b) When I explained my plan of action to him, he did not agree <u>by</u> me.
(c) The principal does not approve <u>for</u> indiscipline.
(d) I need his approval <u>so</u> I can start the work.
(e) An explanation about the evolution of species is given <u>at</u> Chapter 2.
(f) The answers to these questions are given <u>in</u> Page 44.
(g) One fine day, he set <u>for</u> his adventurous trip.
(h) As soon as he entered the room, he set <u>up</u> his heavy bag.
(i) It has been a long time <u>when</u> I saw her.
(j) I have not seen Ravi <u>from</u> ten year now.

SP-05

(iii) Fill in the blanks in the passage given below with the appropriate form of the verb given in brackets. Do not write the passage but write the verbs in correct order. (5)

We decided to travel by car and ...... **(1)** (leave) the house early. We ...... **(2)** (be) on the road for two hours, when our car ...... **(3)** (hit) a stone that ...... **(4)** (lie) in the middle of the road. The car ...... **(5)** (go) off the road but we .... **(6)** (escape) with minor injuries. Had we ...... **(7)** (travel) any faster, we ...... **(8)** (involve) in a serious accident. The mishap .... **(9)** (delay) us but did not ...... **(10)** (damp) our enthusiasm.

Question 4.

Read the passage given below and answer the questions (i), (ii) and (iii) that follow.

(1) The boy found the kites from Japan hidden in a dark passage of the house. Snehamoy helped him take out the kites from the box, lifting each delicately by its **staff** and spread them out on the courtyard.

(2) They fixed the day of celebration for Biswakarma- the god of machines to be their kite-flying day. But first, they'd have to be ready with rolls of line to fly the kites, lines sharpened with a coating of finely **ground** glass to cut those of their rivals. A suitable field must be found, one with a good view of the horizon and free of trees to prevent the lines getting tangled up in the branches. Their hearts pounded at the thought of a kite-fight. Like a sensible teacher, Snehamoy sat the boy down with his exercise book. "If each kite takes five hundred feet of line to fly, how many feet would twenty kites take?" he asked the boy.

The boy frowned, "Only five hundred feet for each kite! What if they get tangled with others during a fight and keep circling away needing more and more?"

(3) The two spent a whole afternoon asking neighbours for empty glass bottles. Snehamoy's aunt smashed them in her kitchen, then ground the shards in a pestle, pricking her thumb in the process. Glue was added to the glass granules and a touch of vermilion dye to have the lines stand out against the blue sky and the clouds. After returning from school, Snehamoy joined the boy in stringing lines from one end of their courtyard to another. Then, like workers, they wrapped their palms in soft cotton cloth, took lavish dips in the pail of abrasive and went from one end of a line to another, carefully applying a **uniform** layer over it. In the end, they sat back in the kitchen and admired the brilliant maze turning their courtyard into a field of red pepper.

(4) For days, pedalling to and fro from school, Snehamoy heard the village buzzing with the impending kite-fight. Rival groups of boys formed teams and were spurred on by a shopkeeper who was offering his regular kites free to anyone who was willing to brave the foreign invasion. Yet on the day of the grand contest, as the first of the Japanese kites came out of the box and heaved by its flyers, went up over the school building, there was a pall of silence. It was a giant Baromon, crashing the helmet of a samurai warrior between its teeth. Scarlet and ochre, it hung still, face up, refused to be cowed by the stiff breeze.

(5) Standing in a circle with the boys, Snehamoy strung the kites, gaze fixed on the sky. Like characters in a play, they made their appearance one by one. The Tsugara whirred like an airplane through a clever loop fixed on its back. The crowd went into a roar over the kabuki faces, which floated in the sky like stained glass windows lit by the afternoon sun. Soon the lines were crossing and tangling up the kites with a steady stream of taunts spurring on the flyers. The boy reached inside the kite box and scooped out more. Instantly the field buzzed with humming and whistling kites shaped as cicadas, gnats, dragonflies and dancing carps. It felt like a carnival and drew the crowd's applause.

*(**Adapted from** 'The Japanese Wife' - Kunal Basil)*

(i) (a) Find a single word from the passage that will exactly replace the underlined word or words in the following sentences. (3)

(1) He carefully carved out the wood to make an intricate statue for his mother.

(2) The vines had grown so densely that they were twisted together, forming a natural barrier around the garden.

(3) It seemed as if everyone was waiting for the performance that was about to happen by the famous singer.

(b) For each of the words given below, choose the correct sentence that uses the same word unchanged in spelling, but with a different meaning from that it carries in the passage. (3)

(1) staff (line 2)

(a) This school has a staff of 30 teachers and 5 Class four employees.
(b) He threw the staff so far away that it was difficult to find.
(c) He tied the cloth to the staff and fixed it on the stone.
(d) All of the above

(2) ground (line 6)
   (a) The Sun dries the moisture on the ground.
   (b) The ground glass was made with a piece of rock
   (c) You need to ground the nut to put it in the mixture
   (d) Please ground the blend before using it.

(3) uniform (line 21)
   (a) I don't like the colour of our school uniform.
   (b) The rows of houses were uniform in appearance.
   (c) Growth has not been uniform across the country.
   (d) Please make sure that every presentation is uniform in appearance.

(ii) Answer the following questions in your own words as briefly as possible.
   (a) How did the kites flown by Snehamoy and the boy add to the atmosphere of joy and brightness? (2)
   (b) How did Snehamoy and the boy decide how much line each kite would need? (2)
   (c) What effect did the impending kite-fight have on the villagers? (2)

(iii) In not more than 100 words of your own, describe the efforts made by Snehamoy and his companion to make the line before the kite-fight. (Failure to keep within the word limit will be penalised.) (8)

Answers *in Topper's Style*

1. (i) Holidays provide an opportunity for people to travel to far off places or to visit a relative's house in a distant town. Everyone plans for their vacation trips. Train journies, being the most convenient, the railway station is found to be the busiest place. It seems as if the whole world gravitates towards the railway station during the holiday season.

During Christmas holidays last year, one of my friends from Lucknow rang me to inform that she was planning to visit Delhi for a week as she had to attend a workshop as well as a wedding. She wanted to know, if I could come to receive her. I enthusiastically volunteered for the prospect of meeting my friend after a gap of 3 years though the thought of the filth and chaos at the station was quite disturbing.

I confirmed her train's arrival time and reached the station 15 minutes before the arrival of her train. When I looked at the display board, I found that the train was running late by one and a half hours due to fog. I had to wait at the station as going back home was not possible or feasible.

I tried to find a place to rest and wait but, to my dismay, the platform was overcrowded with passengers, hawkers, coolies and beggars. There were passengers waiting for trains while some were waiting to receive or drop their near and dear ones. The people had transformed the platforms into vast bedrooms with their luggage tucked under their heads. I wondered how these people could sleep in such filth and noise of hawkers and vendors. The vendors were trying to lure the people to buy edibles. Fluffy poories, steaming hot vegetables, mouth watering samosas, ever boiling tea, coffee and an array of soft drinks were visible everywhere.

Children were tugging at their parent's arms and requesting to eat chips or popcorn. When trying to settle in a corner to eat in peace, a group of monkeys came trooping towards them, causing the children run to another safe place.

Suddenly, there was more commotion at the platform as the Kalka mail arrived at the station. The passengers rushed in making it difficult for the passengers to disembark at the station. The coolies scampered along and pushed the luggage through doors which were already blocked by people. A lady dropped her water bottle and a child began to wail and one could hear hysterical shouting from all the quarters. Suddenly, a lady who had just disembarked from the train yelled that her chain has been snatched, people crowded around her but the snatcher disappeared taking advantage of the crowd. Meanwhile, the newspaper and magazine vendors tried to make their way through the crowd warbling off the names of the magazines.

Beggars limped across or dragged their bodies till they were chased away by railway staff. Finally, after one and a half hour's wait midst ear-piercing noise and confusion, the Lucknow mail arrived. To my relief, my friend waved out from one of the compartments. All in all, while I was excited to meet my friend, the scene at the railway station repulsed me.

(ii) My grandfather was just a child when he and his parents relocated from what is today known as Bangladesh during the Bengal-Bangladesh partition in 1947. This decision of relocation had been initiated by the Indian authorities who, in return for the land that he had left behind there, allotted another large barren land in what was now the capital of independent India - New Delhi. When he shifted, he lived in a secluded area but, in around four years, the area was converted into a beautiful residential complex, full of large houses which we call bungalows. Until last week, it was the only home I had ever known, the place where I had grown up and enjoyed life and now it is to be demolished.

Over the last few years, major changes have taken place in Delhi. With the advent of the Delhi Metro, the very geography of the city has been altered. Suddenly, it has become possible to get from one end of the city to the other in just over an hour and that too in air-conditioned comfort. And, as expected, the spread of the Metro is to expand. It will soon cut through entirely new localities and neighbourhoods. Unfortunately, my ancestral house happens to be in one of those neighbourhoods.

Our entire residential locality happened to be right where a new line of the Delhi Metro was supposed to be. Since it was, of course, impossible for both to simultaneously occupy the space, the locality had to go. The government bought it from all the families for a princely sum and, while this allowed us to buy another house elsewhere, it could do nothing to alleviate the pain we felt at shifting out. I had not been aware of all these ongoings until now when suddenly my mother told me to pack all my belongings as we were to move to Ireland. At first, I was shocked as my father had been pretty stringent about not leaving the ancestral home for his dream job and now he had agreed.

I was not only hurt but also angry. My mother informed me that each and every one in the locality is moving out by the end of the week along with us. So, we all had to hurry.

Four generations of my family had lived in this house and it was suffused with the memories of all the times we had spent here. I was heart-broken at the thought that very soon it would cease to even exist. Even the scope of future that my parents saw in Ireland was no consolation for the loss of memories. But I hope to leave this place with a wish to always cherish my life in the beautiful two-storeyed building I used to call home.

(iii)

For the Motion

'There is sufficiency in this world for man's needs but not man's greed' said Mahatma Gandhi. This quote stands true in the face of the present day world misery and suffering.

I am sure all of you watch TV programmes regularly, particularly entertainment programmes, serials and telecasts of cricket matches on various TV channels. Much like a television set, all of us also have ACs, fridges, mobile phones and what not without which we cannot even imagine our lives. You will find it hard to believe that just 25 years ago there was only one TV channel to watch, i.e. Doordarshan, mobile phones were not popular and even fridges were a rare sight. But, there was a time when man existed without these things and, even when these things were invented, they did not exist in every home as a necessity.

This sheer ignorance of how life was without the presence of luxury gadgets points us to the simple reality of the presence of what was luxury earlier but is a necessity now. The presence of things that better our life like an AC, fridge, etc. creates in man a need to posses them and the inability to do so leads to suffering and pain. It leads to misery which forces a man to lose all of the moral values of the past which we had for so long cherished and loved.

Our ancestors were happy and satisfied without the presence of these things. They did not face any such misery because they could not even imagine the existence of those. The lack of existence then points us towards the lack of need. Thus, we can clearly state our needs, desires and wants because the presence of better things makes us unhappy and causes pain.

This clearly points to the fact that we must learn to control our needs. Our needs become greed which become an obstacle in our lives. In greed, the material world controls us and we join a rat-race which puts us through immense physical and mental stress. The desire to achieve it forces us to leave every moral obligation and responsibility behind, and we become an always unsatisfied selfish humanity.

We all know that excessive desires and needs have always been considered immoral and a violation of divine law. Thus, we all must control our needs and desires to live our life without minimise our suffering and pain.

Against the Motion

To start with, let us point to a scientifically accepted fact. It has been proven time and again that all human beings are born with defined needs which are different for each and every individual. Our needs are dependent on innumerable other facts like age, weight, body structure, lifestyle choices, etc. There is also an acceptance that our needs grow and develop with time and age. A small child always has small and meager needs but a grownup has a much larger and different set of needs.

With this knowledge, the concept of controlling our needs and desires seems to be flawed. While I do believe that becoming selfish and immoral to fulfill our needs is not justified, I also cannot state that needs and desires are always wrong. Our needs and desire for a better future and life motivates and encourages us to become successful which all of us want to be. Without this motivation, life would become purposeless and we would be leading an aimless life after a point. Thus, needs and desires are crucial to existence of all individuals.

Not to forget, even the scientific discoveries and updations that we enjoy in our day-to-day life is a result of the need to know, understand and live in a better equipped world. Then, pain and human suffering are a resultant of something else and not only the human needs.

Fulfillment is the key here. Pain and suffering that a human faces is because of the lack of satisfaction and fulfillment. If we focus on fulfillment, we can easily remove the obstacles that hurt us. After fulfillment of our needs, we must also focus on satisfaction. Man is always on run because after fulfillment of one goal, there is a creation of dissatisfaction and achieving more. Satisfaction and fulfillment in combination with human needs is the ideal combination of living a better life.

Finding joy in simple things, happiness and peace is the main aim of human life. Controlling needs then may make a person mentally sick and disgusted which would have physical impacts. Thus, instead of controlling our needs, we must find ways to satisfy them and march towards a happy and fulfilled life without compromising with our moral values and skills.

(iv) **Memories**

Has it ever happened to you that while listening to a song, you feel nostalgic and are filled to the images of the times when you had played that particular song? It is common for all of us to go through such an experience and feel nostalgic about the memories of the past. These memories are always fresh in our minds and we are overwhelmed with emotions whenever we remember them. But, have we ever wondered what memories are?

Memories are those small incidences that we can never forget and that we treasure throughout life. They are essential parts of our living which connects us to the time that had gone by and help in the development of an individual's personality. They are those moments of our lives that captures the best as well as the worst of an individual's life and, thus, inculcates it into what an individual stands for.

We all have memories that fill us with happiness as well as sadness. It is often perceived that awful memories are not required while cherished memories are indispensable as well as dear to us. I believe that they both are essential for an individual to learn their misstep and improve. While those memories which we often claim as awful and don't ever want to remember help us grow, those which fill us with joy make our lives easy.

Cherished memories are exceptionally huge in our lives. Beloved memories develop our future and perspective. Individuals with great beloved memories are cheerful people. They help in keeping the kid in you alive. In addition, it likewise is a justification for our grins in the middle of grown-up life. This does not mean that a cherished memory is the only thing that characterises an individual however they assume an essential part in one's life. It isn't required that an individual with great memories consistently carries on with a prosperous life while an individual with terrible Memories consistently carries on with a dangerous life. Here and there, repulsive beloved memories make a man more grounded. The purpose of the realities of life is reminded by our memories without fail, be it for joy or for lessons.

Thus, we should all love our memories as they can generally be our friend, our 'joy of isolation.' Simple things hold grave significance when they are from the youth days. The days were liberated from intricacies and loaded with guiltlessness. Thus, they are so close to the heart.

(v) **Films are the Mirror of Society**

Films reflect the society we live in. They show us what' s happening, what people feel and what they care about. They have also played a key role in shaping narratives and opinions of people on what is acceptable and what is not. The Indian film industry, since its inception, has been dedicated towards a portrayal of the society from the grassroots to the urban elite.

Films often tell stories that resonate with people and their real-life experiences. The joys, the highs, the lows and every other emotion that a person feels during the course of their lives finds a place in the movies. Movies could be centered around the dynamic nature of friends or the struggle between the child and parents. Films allows a person to feel as if what he has gone through is normal and that every other person has gone through the same over the course of their life.

Films have also been used to shed light on social issues. They bring attention to issues that are of general importance and need to be talked about. Movies like – *Toilet, Pink, Thappad* have been important to start conversation on such issues publicly. Not just films but documentaries contribute significantly in raising awareness and shedding light on important matters. We, as a generation, consume most of our knowledge through these sources and shape our opinions as well.

Moreover, films also represent the cultural norms of a society. Especially in a country like India which is so culturally rooted, these films have been used to depict customs, traditions and lifestyles of households across the nation. They have led to the beginning of many rituals and also have led to the establishment of trends to be followed. Films have the power to shape stereotypes and societal attitudes. By portraying characters from all walks of life and showcasing such diversity, they create a more empathetic society.

Films act as a dynamic source not only reflecting society but simultaneously also shaping narratives and perceptions. They capture the essence of human beings, shed light on pressing issues and celebrate diversity. We must never underestimate the profound impact of films on our society.

(vi) **The Gift**

The series of events that I will narrate today have been taken from the immediate past of my very own life. The story begins about two months ago when I had given the final exams for my degree in computers. I would become a graduate in about two months' time when the results would be declared. After this, my father wanted me to take over the running of our family's computer sales and service showroom as he wanted to retire and live a peaceful life. In addition, my birthday was also coming up soon for which I knew what I wanted.

For a few weeks, I had been admiring a new model of a Royal Enfield Bullet bike in a dealer's showroom. I had told my father that it was all I wanted for my 22nd birthday. On the morning of my birthday, my father called me into his office in the computer showroom. He first wished me a happy birthday and then told me how much he loved me. He opened his desk drawer, brought out a gift wrapped rectangular box and presented it to me. Curious and somewhat disappointed, I opened the box and found a leather-bound *Bhagwad Gita* in it. I got very angry at him, so I blurted out, "With all your money, you gave me such a book?" Then, I decided to start my own business and stormed out of the house, leaving the gift on his desk.

I went to live with one of my close friends who was staying in an independent flat. After the final exams, I started looking for a job while awaiting my result. However, after a month, I got a call stating that my father had suffered a heart attack and was hospitalised. I rushed to the hospital, but it was too late. He had passed away.

Soon, our family lawyer phoned and told me that in his will my father had left me all his possessions, including ownership of our computer business. With a heavy heart, I went through his papers and soon found gift wrapped the *Bhagwad Gita* he had given me. In tears, I opened the packing and began to turn the pages. Suddenly a key taped to a small envelope dropped from the book. It had a tag with the dealer's name, the same dealer in whose showroom I had seen the bike I wanted. On the tag was the date of my birthday and the words 'Paid in full'.

2. (i) Good morning respected teachers and my dear students. Each year, innumerable lives are lost to road accidents leaving not just physical but also emotional damage in its wake. I have recently observed that there has been a surge in road accidents amongst our students. It is my duty to ensure your safety and to make you aware of the practice of safe driving.

Driving safely is crucial not just for our safety but also for the safety of others on the road. One of the main reasons for road accidents is reckless driving. This covers a wide extent of violations such as speeding, driving while being distracted and driving under influence of alcohol or drugs. These are preventable actions. If people simply adhere to the traffic rules instead of acting recklessly, millions of lives could be saved annually.

Following practices that would ensure our safety should be part of our daily lives. This includes wearing seatbelts, avoiding talking on phones while driving and maintaining the required distance between cars while on road. Even if there is no traffic police or camera to ensure that you follow the rules, you must stick by them and also ensure that others do too.

Following the rules is not enough, we must also be responsible citizens a. If we ever encounter any road accident we must call the ambulance. It is our duty to ensure that any victim of a road accident gets the medical attention they require. Another step to ensure a safe environment is to create awareness. It is a critical step and we must strive forward to create an environment where safety is prioritised. This involves conducting regular educational workshops, seminars and campaigns. It is not just students but also their families that need to be made aware of the devastating consequences of reckless driving.

The need for action is upon us. We must actively engage in the cause of creating a safe driving environment. This commitment starts with each one of us taking personal esponsibility for our actions. As students, you have a unique opportunity to set an example for your peers and contribute to a safer community.

In conclusion, let us all pledge to be more vigilant, responsible and conscientious drivers. Remember, the life you save by driving safely could be your own or someone you love. Together, we can make a significant difference and ensure that our roads are safe for everyone.

Thank you for your attention.

(ii) **Proposal for Visiting an Orphanage**

Heading To make children understand compassion, empathy and kindness with the help of donations.

Objectives To eliminate the loneliness and boredom of the children for a day and to give them a feel of happiness with our games, fun and food.

List of Measures

- Students of Classes VI to X will be a part of this visit.
- A contribution of ₹ 100 will be collected from the students as the cost of food and transportation.
- Students will also be asked for donations in the forms of stationary, clothes and books.
- Students will be preparing a humorous skit as well as games for the orphans.
- The students will try to connect with the children through games and exchange of stories.
  We hope that this proposal will be accepted, soon and our aim to provide some moments of joy and love to the children will be fulfilled.

3. (i) (a) How long I shall stay is doubtful.
(b) She was so full that she could not have another meal.
(c) Ranjeet asked Sheela why she didn't take the advice of her parents in that matter.
(d) It has been over two months since Rahul has been to school.
(e) The book was lost by me.

(ii) (a) upon (b) with (c) of (d) before
(e) in (f) on (g) out (h) aside
(i) since (j) for

(iii) 1. left 2. had been 3. hit 4. lay
5. went 6. escaped 7. travelled
8. would have been involved 9. delayed 10. dampen

4. (i) (a) (1) delicately (2) tangled (3) impending
(b) (1) (d) All of the above
(2) (a) The Sun dries the moisture on the ground.
(3) (a) I don't like the colour of our school uniform.

(ii) (a) The kites flown by Snehamoy and the boy added to the atmosphere of joy and brightness as the field buzzed with the humming and whistling of kites shaped as cicadas, gnats, dragonflies and dancing carps. The kites added to the feel of the carnival and drew the crowd's applause.
(b) Snehamoy and the boy sat down with an exercise book to calculate how much line each kite needed. Snehamoy suggested five hundred feet for each kite but the boy suggested that more line was needed for the twenty kites.
(c) The villagers were quite excited about the kite fighting. Rival groups of boys formed teams and were encouraged by a local shopkeeper who was offering his regular kites for free to stop the invasion of the rival kites.

(iii) Snehamoy and the boy made elaborate arrangements to make the line before the kite-fight. They calculated how much line they would need for the kites to fly. Then they collected empty bottles and broke them to be grounded into powder. Glue and a touch of vermilion was added to the granules to make paste for the line. Together, they strung lines in their courtyard and then wrapped their palms in soft cotton cloth, took lavish dips in the abrasive mix and went from one end of a line to another, carefully applying a uniform layer on the line.

SQP Code : **PB-6/10** Series ***i*-Succeed 6-25/10** Roll No. | | | | | | | | |

Sample Question Paper 06

English Language 12th (Code 801)

General Instructions

1. You are allowed additional 15 minutes for only reading the question paper.
2. You must NOT start writing during reading time.
3. It has four questions in all.
4. Answer all questions.
5. You are advised to spend not more than 45 minutes on Question 1, 55 minutes on Question 2, 30 minutes on Question 3 and 50 minutes on Question 4.
6. You should begin each answer on a fresh page.
7. The intended marks for questions are given in brackets [ ].

Time : 3 Hrs.

Max. Marks : 80

Question 1.

Write a composition (in approximately 400-450 words) on any one of the following subjects. (20)

(You are reminded that you will be rewarded for orderly and coherent presentation of material, use of appropriate style and general accuracy of spelling, punctuation and grammar.)

(i) 'Society is influenced more by show than by substance.' Relate an incident from your experience which brings out the truth of this statement.

(ii) A foreigner will be visiting you for a fortnight and you wish to introduce him/her to 'Incredible India' during that time. Give an account of your plans.

(iii) Express your views either for or against the motion "Crime-based serials on TV lead to a reduction in crime."

(iv) Money

(v) "Success depends on character and not on opportunity." Express your views on the statement.

(vi) Write an original story which has for its ending... I just exclaimed, 'Truth is Stranger than Fiction'.

Question 2.

(i) There is a reputed institution providing a prestigious degree in Instrumental Music- Piano. Write a statement of purpose so that you can be favourably be considered for admission in about 300 words.

Introduction-what you wish to study and why-work experience-importance of this institution-what you hope to do in future-conclusion (15)

(ii) As the head of the Students' Wing of the RWA of your colony, you have been given the responsibility of organising the children of your colony and undertaking a rally against firecrackers. Write a proposal in about 150 words stating the steps you would take to effectively organise this Anti-firecrackers Diwali Rally. (10)

Question 3.

Answer sections **(i)**, **(ii)** and **(iii)**

(i) Rewrite the following sentences according to the instructions given after each of them in the brackets. (50)

(a) Sachin is an outstanding sportsman and a good artist.
Use: (besides.........also............)

(b) Mother said to Paul, "A courier came for you yesterday."
Begin: (Mother told Paul that ....)

(c) As soon as the minister took the oath, the spectators started applauding.
Use: (......than.........)

(d) You must work hard to earn well.
Begin: (If..........................)

(e) The lawyer examined the documents with utmost care.
End: (.....................by the lawyer.)

(ii) In the following sentences, replace the **INCORRECT** underlined words to make the sentences more meaningful and grammatically correct. (Do not copy the sentences.) (5)

(a) After the argument, his friends turned after him.
(b) Ramesh turned for his father for help.
(c) The Headmaster will look at the cheating case.
(d) I look up at my grandfather for what he has achieved.
(e) She takes over her mother.
(f) Ramesh has taken by computers like a duck to water.
(g) Will you entrust him for that message?
(h) The programme ran after six hours.
(i) Do not put up till tomorrow what you can do today.
(j) I put over at my friend's house for the night.

(iii) Fill in the blanks in the passage given below with the appropriate form of the verb given in brackets. Do not write the passage but write the verbs in correct order. (5)

One day, a millionaire went to a hotel in New York and .... **(1)** (ask) for the cheapest room they .... **(2)** (be). "What .... **(3)** (be) the price of the room?", he .... **(4)** (ask). The manager .... **(5)** (tell) him, "Is that the cheapest room you .... **(6)** (be)? I .... **(7)** (stay) by myself and only .... **(8)** (need) a small room." The manager said, "Why do you choose a poor room like that? Your son always .... **(9)** (stay) in our most expensive room." 'Yes', said the millionaire, "but his father .... **(10)** (be) a wealthy man, mine is not."

Question 4.

Read the passage given below and answer the questions (i), (ii) and (iii) that follow.

(1) I could hear the squeaking that heralded the evening arrival of the **bats**. I listened to the noises of the approaching night. Every day my hearing grew sharper. I was learning to filter out whatever I did not need to listen to and giving no **sign** that I could hear everything that went on in the house.

(2) I could not sleep. The air was heavy and still, the moon hidden behind thick **banks** of cloud. Lord Otori was sound asleep. I did not want to leave the house I'd come to love so much, but I seemed to be bringing nothing but trouble to it. Perhaps, it would be better for everyone if I just vanished in the night.

(3) Now, I heard the hiss of hot water as the bath was prepared, the clatter of dishes from the kitchen, the sliding sigh of the cook's knife, a dog barking two streets away and the sounds of feet on the wooden bridges on the canals. I knew the sounds of the house, day and night, in sunshine and under the rain.

This evening I realised I was always listening for something more. I was waiting too. For what?

(4) I began to wonder if I could get out of the house without setting the dogs barking and arousing the guards. I started consciously listening for the dogs. Usually, I heard them bark on and off throughout the night but I'd learned to distinguish their barks and to ignore them. I set my ears for them but heard nothing. Then I started listening for the guards: the sound of a foot on stone or a whispered conversation. Nothing. Sounds that should have been there were missing from the night's familiar web.

(5) Now I was wide-awake, straining my ears to hear. There came the slightest of sounds, hardly more than a tremor, between the window and the ground.

(6) For a moment I thought it was the Earth-shaking, as it so often did. Another tiny tremble followed, then another. Someone was climbing up the side of the house.

(7) My first instinct was to yell out, but cunning took over. I rose from the mattress and crept silently to Lord Otrori's side. I knelt beside him and whispered in his ear, "Lord Otori, someone is outside."

(8) He woke instantly and then reached for the sword and knife that lay beside him. I gestured to the window. The faint tremor came again.

(9) Lord Otori passed the knife to me and stepped to the wall. I moved to the other side of the window. We waited for the assassin to climb in.

(10) Step by step he came up the wall, stealthy and unhurried, as if he had all the time in the world. We waited for him with the same patience.

(11) He paused on the still to take out the knife he planned to use on us and then stepped inside. Lord Otori took him in a stranglehold. The intruder wriggled backwards. I leaped at him and the three of us fell into the garden like a flurry of fighting cats.

SP-06

(12) The man fell first, across the stream, striking his head on a boulder. Lord Otori landed on his feet. My fall was broken by one of the shrubs. The intruder groaned, tried to rise, but slipped back into the water.

(13) "Get a light," Lord Otori said.

(14) I ran to the house, took a light that still burned in one of the candle stands and carried it back to the garden.

(15) The assassin had died without regaining consciousness. It turned out he had a poison pellet in his mouth and had crushed it as he fell. He was dressed in black, with no marking on his clothes. I held the light over him. There was nothing to tell us who he was.

(***Adapted from*** *Tales of the Otori by Lian Hearn*)

(i) (a) Find a single word from the passage that will exactly replace the underlined word or words in the following sentences. (3)

(1) The lion hid behind the <u>large rock</u> keeping watch on its prey.

(2)The stalker <u>moved slowly and carefully</u> behind its target waiting for the perfect time to strike.

(3) The police finally apprehended the murderer and put him behind bars for his crimes.

(b) For each of the words given below, choose the correct sentence that uses the same word unchanged in spelling, but with a different meaning from that which it carries in the passage. (3)

(1) bats (line 1)
- (a) All the players were given new bats as a gift from the celebrated player.
- (b) Jackson found that fruit bats are a creature of the morning.
- (c) The largest bat colony has been found in Africa.
- (d) Suraj found about a 100 bats lying around in the region.

(2) sign (line 3)
- (a) I saw the sign of the palace earlier so I think we are on the right path.
- (b) I urgently need you to sign this document as it needs to be submitted today.
- (c) His silence is sign of his anger regarding the event.
- (d) Jayesh went to the market hoping to get the sign of Raashi.

(3) banks (line 5)
- (a) The banks were crowded with stairs for boats.
- (b) We found the boys at the banks of the river.
- (c) There are many private banks in India.
- (d) The banks are considered to be holy.

(ii) Answer the following questions in your own words as briefly as possible.

(a) Why couldn't the narrator sleep? What could the narrator hear as he was lying down? (2)

(c) When did he realise that there was something wrong? (2)

(d) How did the narrator and Lord Otori overpower the intruder? (2)

(iii) Describe the incident of the assassination attempt that took place during the night, in not more than 100 words (Paragraphs 4 to 15). Failure to keep within the word limit will be penalised. (8)

Answers in Topper's Style

1. (i) There is just no place for factual plain speaking in today's highly materialistic society. It is not uncommon to find friends bragging about their royal or star connections to impress others. This is most blatantly practiced in the corporate world, especially in advertising products or services. Companies resort to gimmicks to get noticed and gain popularity. They make tall claims about their product or services that are not in conformity to what they offer.

Thus, one finds star personalities from Bollywood or the sports' world, endorsing cars and motor cycles. One might even find a bearded celebrity glorifying a particular brand of shaving cream. Advertisers use brand ambassadors who have no relation to the product in an attempt to catch the attention of the consumer. This shows that the present 'Society is influenced more by show than by substance'.

I had a firsthand experience of the truth of this statement during the Navratri festival last year. 'The Times', a renowned event management group of Delhi, organised an event titled, 'Dance with the Stars'. The programme was a Dandiya dance event held in the lawns of a prestigious hotel of the city.

Renowned stars like Aishwariya Rai, Urmila Matondkar, Raveena Tandon, Salman Khan and my favourite hero Hritik Roshan, were to grace the occasion. The hype enabled them to sell the tickets priced at ₹ 3000/- each. I managed to get a ticket for the show after waiting in the queue for two hours. I had rejected on attending the local dandiyaras with my childhood friends for this event. So, I had high expectations of the event.

On reaching the hotel, I found a huge crowd waiting at the gate to catch a glimpse of the stars. Some young boys watched in envy as I made my way through the brightly lit entrance. The show, as with all such star studded programmes, began an hour late. The local orchestra 'Guys' regaled the crowd with some of the best pop music. The glamorous dancers with dandia in their hands, danced well into the night but there was no trace of the 'Stars'.

Sonia, the VJ of Channel V, heightened the anxiety by announcing that the stars were about to arrive. This continued well past midnight but there was no trace of the promised stars. At about half past twelve, Sonia introduced Johnny Lever and Namrata to the audience regretting that others could not come because of pressing engagements.

It was a big letdown. The crowd grew restless and vented vent to their anger by booing and hooting the organisers. Normalcy returned with great difficulty as Johnny Lever with his characteristic jokes made light of the situation. The three-hour programme just lasted for an hour, after which the crowd just thinned out.
I returned home feeling cheated to the core. I cursed myself for having spent a princely amount on an event that was just no better than the jam sessions in school.

Indeed, my decision to participate in the event was influenced more by show. I was carried away with the advertisement 'Dance with the Stars' rather than the joy and gaiety of the dandiyaras.

(ii) There are some parts of the world which once visited would become so memorable that you can never forget them. India is one such place. One can be stunned by the richness of the land, its lush beauty, exotic architecture and historical monuments. Each region of India has unique physical features, soil, type of climate and wildlife. When the natural beauty is mingled with diverse culture, the resultant harmony presents a majestic sparkling picture reflecting each destination in its uniqueness, i.e. showing Incredible India!

I got the opportunity to show this beauty of my nation to one of my clients when she visited India for a fortnight. The client was based in USA. I was told to plan her trip and to do it in such a way that she could visit the most exotic places all over India and get a glimpse of our great cultural heritage and natural beauty.
I had a great responsibility as I had to show India at its best. I decided to put some extra efforts to give my client a real experience of 'Incredible India'.

I logged on to the yatra.com website and after many hours of research finally drew up an interesting itinerary for my client. I decided that Delhi will be her first destination. During the two-day journey, the plan was to take her to Red Fort, Jama Masjid, Qutub Minar, Lotus Temple, Akshardham Temple, Garden of five senses, National Art Gallery and Siri Fort Auditorium where she could see enjoy the beauty of Indian architecture while also learning about our nation's rich culture. I had also planned to take her to Dilli Haat and Central Cottage emporium to shop Indian handicrafts and clothes for her friends and family.

After this, she would be taken to a trip to Golden triangle : Agra, Jaipur and Udaipur. The plan was chalked out to first go to Agra and see the grandeur of the Taj Mahal, Fatehpur Sikri and Sikandra Fort. Next, we will go to Jaipur and visit the Amer Fort and the Jantar-Mantar. The plan was also to visit the local market famous for semi-precious jewellery, authentic Rajasthani handicrafts and clothes of block prints and Sanganeri prints. Next was a visit to Udaipur, the city of lakes and beautiful gardens also famous for marble statues and mandirs.

After this, we will take a flight and go to Darjeeling and Meghalaya. The mesmerising range of Himalayas, sunrise at the Tiger point, the Mirik lake, Kalimpong and the Orchid gardens are worth visiting. On our way back, we could make a one-day stop at Kolkata and then take a direct flight to Chennai in Tamil Nadu where we would enjoy the southern cuisine along with the clear beaches and the elaborate temples.

The trip would be tiring and still we would not be able to see many unique features of the nation. A fortnight is a very short period to discover the 'Incredible India'.

(iii) **For the Motion**

Television crime dramas and shows are becoming very popular all over the world. This popularity is not bound to a certain age group, rather all the television viewers like these shows. With this increasing popularity, people in the media industry all over the world are coming up with new shows in innumerable fields. Be it thriller based crime shows or shows related to social taboos, the television industry does have a great impact on our society.

Keeping this fact in mind, more and more crime based shows are coming up to enthrall the masses. These crime serials play a positive role in society by creating awareness and spreading information regarding crimes. The make people aware of crimes taking place in the immediate surroundings and how they can stay safe in such an environment. Consequently, this knowledge can definitely saves many lives by enabling them to take certain precautions.

The end result of all the shows related to crime is more awareness and information that would reduce criminal tendencies. There will be some exceptions where individuals develop an unhealthy obsession that isolates them from society but this is just as likely to occur with any form of entertainment.

Also, the crime shows reflect the positive role of law enforcement agencies while alerting the people regarding such incidences. It shows how every time a crime takes place, the law enforcement of our country is ready to take charge and catch the criminal. Such a representation of law agencies creates an image of fear and a warning to those who have the criminal tendencies.

Instead of inducing crime, the shows give a message that crime never pays and will always take one down. Criminal tendencies are repressed at the very start and a positive image prevails.

Against the Motion

With the prevalence and popularity of crime shows both on television and other media forms, one cannot help but state that these television shows are linked to the ever increasing crimes. I agree that these shows have a great positive impact on the minds of people regarding the law enforcement agencies. However, one cannot deny the reality that we as common people accept that there are innumerable criminals out there who are still committing serious crimes and are inducing criminal tendencies.

The trending crime shows and even movies show that criminals live a lavish lifestyle and enjoy their life to the fullest without any fear. Such a representation moulds the behaviour of the child and effects child brain negatively. Coupled with the knowledge of the free criminals, such children are more and more attracted to the world of crime and think of themselves as fearless.

These shows also give new and different ideas to evil minds to commit crime. More importantly, many criminals find loopholes in the laws through which they can evade punishment by watching these crime serials. They start believing that they too can live such a life without any fear of being caught and punished by the law.

While we accept that the shows do produce a positive impact, it is also necessary to accept that this impact is fairly limited. In addition, it is not just about one particular show but about innumerable such shows that exist on TV and over the various OTT platforms. The large number of such shows viewed by children is also at fault. Without any filter or adult supervision, children get desensitised towards violence and get stuck in the negative mindset product by the shows and hence are pushed into the world of crime.

Instead of producing the positive impact it was supposed to create, it creates a negative impact that destroys the future of not only the child but also the nation.

(iv) **Money**

Money, as a concept and medium of exchange, has evolved significantly over millennia, shaping economies, societies, and human interactions. Its history traces back to ancient civilisations where barter systems and commodities were used before the advent of standardised currency.

The concept of money began with the emergence of trade and commerce in ancient societies. Early civilisations such as Mesopotamia, Egypt and China utilised commodities like grain, livestock and precious metals as mediums of exchange. These items had intrinsic value and were accepted in trade due to their usefulness and scarcity.

The transition to standardised currency marked a significant development in the history of money. The first coins appeared in ancient Lydia (modern-day Turkey) around the 7th century BCE. These coins were stamped with symbols or images to indicate their authenticity and value, facilitating easier trade and commerce across regions.

In ancient Rome, the denarius became a widely recognised currency, used for transactions and taxation within the vast Roman Empire. The stability and uniformity of Roman currency contributed to economic prosperity and facilitated the expansion of trade routes and cultural exchange.

During the Middle Ages, various forms of currency emerged across Europe including coins minted by feudal lords and merchants. However, the lack of standardised currencies and widespread counterfeit practices hindered economic stability until the Renaissance period when banking institutions and paper money began to emerge.

The modern concept of money took shape with the establishment of central banks, national currencies, and the adoption of fiat money backed by the authority of governments. In the 20th century, the Bretton Woods Agreement established a system of fixed exchange rates pegged to the US dollar, laying the foundation for international monetary stability and economic cooperation.

Today, money plays a crucial role in global economies as a medium of exchange, unit of account and store of value. It enables individuals and businesses to conduct transactions, invest in assets, and accumulate wealth. Financial systems including banks, stock markets, and digital payment platforms, facilitate the circulation and management of money on a global scale.

Moreover, money influences social dynamics by shaping social hierarchies, consumer behaviour, and aspirations for material wealth. The pursuit of financial success and security motivates individuals to work, invest, and save, contributing to economic growth and development. However, disparities in wealth distribution, economic inequalities, and financial instability remain persistent challenges that impact societies worldwide.

In conclusion, the history and significance of money underscore its transformative impact on human societies and economies. From its origins in ancient trade to its role in modern globalised economies, money continues to evolve and adapt to changing economic and technological landscapes. Understanding the complexities of money provides insights into its profound influence on human behaviour, societal structures, and the pursuit of prosperity in contemporary times.

(v) "So shines a good deed in a naughty world", said William Shakespeare implying that a person with a good character stands out in the bad and selfish world. Success to such a person comes sooner than later in the chosen field of activity.

Opportunity is basically the favourable juncture of circumstances and success is the fulfilling of a given task or goal. The favourable juncture of circumstances comes to a person blessed with a good character. One's purity of thought and relentless effort toward one's goal do not go unnoticed in the society. Hence, sooner or later opportunity knocks at such a person's door. Thomas Edison rightly said, "Opportunity is missed by most people because it is dressed in overalls and looks like work."

Success has different connotations for different people. For some, accumulation of wealth could be a barometer of success while for others it could be the exercise of power, authority, knowledge or social status. In the absence of character, one may become successful by clutching at opportunities using fair or foul means but such glory is usually short-lived and transitory. We have before us the example of Hitler who was a mere soldier in the German army. He rose to power as the Fuehrer seizing every opportunity that came his way. However, his skewed personality brought about his downfall and his country to ruin in the Second World War. Such opportunists may scale great heights but their downfall is as steep as their meteoric rise.

Character helps optimise on the opportunity. It is a ladder to achieve one's goal in life. The pleasant and wholesome personality of such a person catches the attention of and is appreciated by others. This recognition brings opportunities which one seizes with both hands. One's disciplined approach in life enables one to make the best use of it to achieve the goal. When success bears the stamp of one's character, it becomes more stable and lasting.

History is replete with many illustrious men of character who became great leaders, often changing the destiny of their nation. Mahatma Gandhi, by dint of his character, challenged the mighty British Empire. He did not have to look for an opportunity to come his way but opportunity was thrust on him and he became immortal as the Father of the Nation.

Albert Einstein acknowledging the importance of character said, "Most people say that it is the intellect which makes a great scientist. They are wrong, it is the character." Indeed, character is the touchstone for success.

(vi) **Truth is Stranger than Fiction**

My friends, Chester and Shahnaj, lived in neighbouring housing complexes in Mumbai. They both used to leave for their work almost at the same time and catch the same bus. They noticed each other. In the beginning, they did not speak to each other and acknowledged that they lived in same society but slowly things changed.

They became friends. In the evening after work, they started spending time together. Chester was Christian and Shahnaj was Muslim. However, they were not orthodox in their views and had common views on most of the matters despite their different religions. "Do you go to church every Sunday?" asked Shahnaj one day while they were sitting at Chowpati and enjoying the ice-cream. "Not very regularly" replied Chester. "But, I do visit it sometimes." "Do you observe Ramzan?" asked Chester, "Yes I do. But, to tell you frankly, I am not that regular", Shahnaj replied.

One day, Chester did not go to office. Shahnaj looked for him but as he was nowhere to be found, she thought he must have gone to meet his parents at Hyderabad. In the evening, she rang up Chester and came to know that he was ill and was in his flat for last 3 days. He had developed typhoid. That very evening, Shahnaj went to see him. Chester had grown very weak. Shahnaj took good care of him, gave him timely medicines and food. Chester was very grateful and thanked her immensely.

"Why did you not call someone from home?" Shahnaj enquired.

Chester revealed then that his parents were quite old and lived in Hyderabad. He did not have anyone else. He also told her that they were not his biological parents. They had adopted him when he was four or five years old. He was an orphan. She was very curious to know the other details. Chester told her that he lived in a village in Odisha. Due to cyclones, his village was completely destroyed. His parents also died in the cyclone. He also told Shahnaj that his parents were Hindus. A childless Christian couple adopted him as he had nobody to look after him.

Shahnaj was dumb-struck and what she revealed to Chester was unbelievable. She told him that she also belonged to a small village in Odisha and her parents were also killed in the same cyclone She was an orphan and was adopted by a Muslim couple who gave her lot of love. When she disclosed the name of her village, both were very excited as they were born in the same village and fate had played the same type of joke with them.

They both decided to marry and received their parents' blessing. Hearing their story, I just exclaimed, 'truth indeed is stranger than fiction'.

2. (i) My life's passion has been music ever since I was old enough to sing. As I have grown and matured, I have been on a constant quest to explore new musical vistas and hone my own technical and composition skills. By luck, I found my love for piano. My love for piano started when I heard a child playing it masterfully in the airport waiting lounge. The ways his fingers moved and the boy was entranced captivated me and, soon, I joined my daily classes for piano. Now, having earned a degree in music and acquired teaching experience, I desire to further hone my musical talent overseas. The music education in my native country is somewhat limited and not nearly as open or developed as it is in France, which is why I am attracted to the enriching, inspiring environment of your master's programme. In addition, I look forward to experiencing a new culture and interacting with diverse groups of people, which will broaden both my personal and musical horizons considerably.

As a young child, I often played the piano and sang songs with my mother. After learning the basics of piano, I soon began playing it by ear and gradually began adding my own flair to songs. I was fortunate to have a mother who supported my passion for music. She got me a composition teacher which led me to focus on composition in junior and senior high school. During this period, I mainly played classical music which gave me a good foundation for my university-level studies. The numerous undergraduate classes I took on harmony, theory, music analysis, counterpoint and composition opened my eyes to the vast possibilities I could explore in the musical world.

My experiences have molded me into a multi-talented musician with a keen understanding of my own strengths and interests. This is why I feel well prepared to enter your majors programme of music. If accepted, I will devote my efforts to enriching my knowledge of music and composition and I hope to focus on the area of contemporary music. I understand that studying overseas will present me with certain challenges but, based on my past accomplishments and struggles, I know that I have what it takes to overcome these and excel. After completing my studies, I plan to return to my country and seek a teaching position with the goal of nurturing the next generation of musicians and inspiring others as my teachers inspired me.

Thanks and regards

Abhishek Agarwal

(ii) **Proposal for Setting Up an Anti-firecrackers Diwali Rally**

Heading To set up a rally against firecracker due to the upcoming occasion of diwali to help the children learn the importance of the need to stop pollution caused by crackers.

Objectives The anti-firecrackers rally would promote the values of discipline and respect for the environment in children, and educate and sensitise them about the importance of cleanliness for a healthy, socially responsible, economically dynamic and progressive nation.

List of Measures

- Everyone, will join the rally which would take the round of the colony while shouting slogans and making people aware of how firecrackers affects the environment.
- Charts and banners with motivational quotes informing residents about the need to stop bursting firecrackers will be prepared.
- Distributing flyers to the people of the locality and explaining to them how we can celebrate an eco-friendly diwali.
- Arranging refreshment for the children.

We hope that the proposal will be accepted so that the Cleanliness Drive can be organised well.

3. (i) (a) Besides being an outstanding sportsman, Sachin is a good artist.

(b) Mother told Paul that a courier had come for him the previous day.

(c) No sooner did the minister take the oath than the spectators started applauding.

(d) If you want to earn well, you must work hard.

(e) The documents were examinedwith utmost care by the lawyer.

(ii) (a) against (b) to (c) into (d) to

(e) after (f) to (g) with (h) for

(i) off (j) up

(iii) 1. asked 2. had 3. is 4. asked
5. told 6. have 7. shall stay 8. need
9. stays 10. is

4. (i) (a) (1) boulder (2) crept (3) assassin

(b) (1) (a) All the players were given new bats as a gift from the celebrated player.

(2) (b) I urgently need you to sign this document as it needs to be submitted today.

(3) (c) There are many private banks in India.

(ii) (a) The narrator could not sleep because he was troubled. He was debating whether he should leave the house he loved so much because he seemed to bring nothing but trouble for Lord Otori.

(b) The narrator felt that there was something wrong when he tried to listen to the guards. Much to his surprise, the familiar and usual sounds of the guards were missing. Instead, he could feel the Earth shaking and trembling indicating that someone was trying to climb up the side of the house.

(c) When someone was trying to enter the house secretly, the narrator and Lord Otori planned on capturing the assassin. As the man stepped inside, Lord Otori had him in a stranglehold. As the narrator lept on the intruder, the three men fell into the garden. The intruder fell in the water and was thus overpowered.

(iii) The narrator could not sleep at night. He had heard strange sounds that kept him awake. However, at one point, he felt that the Earth was shaking and noticed an intruder outside. He was an assassin. The narrator and Lord Otori planned to overpower him. They attacked and pushed him into the water. The assassin hit his head on a boulder. Later on, they discovered that the man had a poison pellet in his mouth and had crushed it as he fell. He died immediately because of the poison.

SQP Code : **PB-7/10**	Series ***i*-Succeed 7-25/10**	Roll No.

Sample Question Paper 07

English Language 12th (Code 801)

General Instructions

1. You are allowed additional 15 minutes for only reading the question paper.
2. You must NOT start writing during reading time.
3. It has four questions in all.
4. Answer all questions.
5. You are advised to spend not more than 45 minutes on Question 1, 55 minutes on Question 2, 30 minutes on Question 3 and 50 minutes on Question 4.
6. You should begin each answer on a fresh page.
7. The intended marks for questions are given in brackets [ ].

Time : 3 Hrs.

Max. Marks : 80

Question 1.

Write a composition (in approximately 400-450 words) on any one of the following subjects. (20)

(You are reminded that you will be rewarded for orderly and coherent presentation of material, use of appropriate style and general accuracy of spelling, punctuation and grammar.)

(i) Describe one embarrassing/awkward incident about you that your school life that you will always remember.

(ii) You had a nerve-wrecking experience when you fell into a ditch with a snake which was later identified as Cobra. Narrate the incident and how you came out of that situation.

(iii) 'Government's ban on dissection of animals in laboratories is justified.' Write **for** or **against** the topic.

(iv) Dreams

(v) 'Actions speak louder than words.' Express your views on the given statement.

(vi) Write an original story beginning with the words– 'I knew at once that the blue envelope was from her. My hands trembled as I reached for it … .

Question 2.

(i) Write an article in about 300 words on "Indian Population Explosion: A Grave Challenge" for your school newspaper. You can use the following clues (15)
Root cause of challenges- huge population- crises- limited resources- illiteracy- lack of awareness- neutralise economic growth- immense pressure on nature- slowing development.

(ii) As a member of the Student Council of your school, you have been given the responsibility of setting up a Physics Club. Write a proposal in about 150 words stating the steps you would take to successfully establish this particular club. (10)

Question 3.

Answer sections **(i)**, **(ii)** and **(iii)**

(i) Rewrite the following sentences according to the instructions given after each of them in the brackets. (5)

(a) Though it was a cloudy day, the temperature was 45°C.
Begin: (Despite..........................)

(b) They are demolishing the entire block of flats.
End: (..................................by them.)

(c) Anil thought the examination would be held later.
Begin: (Anil was of the opinion...)

(d) I do not like this food as much as you do.
Use: (...........more..........................)

(e) Raju failed in the examination yet he was not upset.
Begin: (In spite of ....)

(ii) In the following sentences, replace the **INCORRECT** underlined words to make the sentences more meaningful and grammatically correct. (Do not copy the sentence) (5)

(a) Let us talk <u>for</u> them tomorrow about their homework.

(b) The Principal warned us <u>of</u> bullying.

(c) Manoj was not at home when his grand father passed <u>by</u>.

(d) When we visited Dalhousie, we passed <u>on</u> the house in which we had lived twenty years ago.

(e) Most students benefit <u>with</u> interactions with fellow students outside school hours.

(f) In the Middle Ages, books were written <u>from</u> a variety of subjects.

(g) He had promised her that he would come to the party but he didn't turn <u>away</u>.

(h) I was forced to turn <u>back</u> Maya's invitation as I was going to be out of town the following week.

(i) Rashi has applied <u>to</u> a scholarship in an American university.

(j) There is no point in going <u>above</u> the answer now.

SP-07

(iii) Fill in the blanks in the passage given below with the appropriate form of the verb given in brackets. Do not write the passage but write the verbs in correct order. (5)

As I entered the room, the first thing that .... **(1)** (strike) me as odd, was the candle still .... **(2)** (burn) on the table. The curtains had been .... **(3)** (draw) back and the room was bright. No one in their right mind .... **(4)** (keep) a candle .... **(5)** (burn) in broad daylight. The large French windows overlooked the lawn .... **(6)** (bath) in sunlight. Marie had probably .... **(7)** (catch) my odd stare at the table and so ....**(8)** (move) over and blew the candle out. She then .... **(9)** (glance) at the windows and .... **(10)** (go) over to open them.

Question 4.

Read the passage given below and answer the questions (i), (ii) and (iii) that follow.

(1) I often went to the lagoon, which has a four-fathom bank where the tababa (tiger shark) muster in hundreds for a day or two every month. Offshore at rising tide, you can watch their great striped bodies sliding and swooping with arrogant ease not six feet under your keel. They range in length from nine to fourteen feet, with an occasional giant of eighteen feet. Their hideous size contrasts nightmarishly with the slack grace of their movements. 5

(2) Thirty-five years ago, the Gilbertese were beginning to use steel hooks for shark-fishing but many still claimed that the old-style twelve-inch wooden hook, trained to the right shape on the living ironwood tree was the only thing for tiger shark. The shark hunter's gaff was a glorious **club** with a ten-pound stone for its head. He fished from a canoe not much longer than a man, with the line made **last** to it. When a big shark took the hook, the craft lurched suddenly and started careering round in mad circles or it bounced insanely up and down or it zigzagged like a misdirected rocket, the fisherman holding on grimly.

(3) Half a dozen cockleshells milling round like that, without visible means of propulsion, made a wildly eccentric sight from the shore. But the fury of a tiger shark's struggles soon **exhausted** it and it floated limply to the surface. Then the fisherman hauled the spent brute cautiously alongside and letting out one piercing howl of pleasure, cracked it on the nose with his club.

(4) Usually safety first is the rule when tiger sharks are about, but the feat of one Tarawa man, Teriakai, became a matter of official record. His vital, stocky frame was the equal of a giant's work. Whenever there was a special job to be done, we always chose Teriakai to do it Thus, when the captain and chief engineer of a visiting steamer wanted to go out for a sail in threatening weather, we sent Teriakai along to look after them.

(5) A Northerly storm caught Teriakai and his friends and capsized their boat, spilling them into the lagoon eight miles from land, with tiger shark all round.

(6) Teriakai immediately hacked the mainsail adrift; buoyed at head and foot by its spars, it made a fine bag under water. 'Stay inside this,' he said to the captain and engineer and the tababa won't smell you. Then he put down the anchor and started for shore to get help. 'If I get past the tababa' he said, 'We shall perhaps be meeting again.'

(7) He swam straight at the tiger sharks - the captain and engineer watched him - and the devils let him through. Teriakai told me afterwards, "If you stay still in the sea, or swim away in fear, the tababa will charge you. If you swim without fear towards them, they will be afraid and leave you in peace." So he chose his shark, swam lull speed towards it and lo! the line melted away before him. There was nothing to it - except a conarge that passes belief.

(8) The swift night of the equator fell. In the welter of waves, Teriakai missed his direction and swam into a maze of reefs off the coast. The breaking seas flung him on cruel edges, rolled him over splintering coral-branches, but he got through, still conscious, swam a mile to shore, walked two more to a white trader's house and collapsed on the veranda.

*(**Adapted from** 'A Pattern of Islands' by Arthur Grimble)*

SP-07

(i) (a) Find a single word from the passage that will exactly replace the underlined word or words in the following sentences. (3)

(1) The cheetah, known for its incredible speed and grace, is a remarkable <u>animal</u>.

(2) The storm raged <u>in an unrelenting manner</u>, battering the coastline with powerful winds and torrential rain.

(3) The plane began to <u>move in a turbulent fashion</u> as it encountered severe weather.

(b) For each of the words given below, choose the correct sentence that uses the same word unchanged in spelling, but with a different meaning from that which it carries in the passage. (3)

(1) club (line 9)

(a) The Lions Club distributed blankets to the poor on the New Year Eve.

(b) You need to tie the cloth to the end of the long club.

(c) The club was not sharp and so could not be used.

(d) The aim of the game is to fetch your team's cloth/flag from the club.

(2) last (line 10)
  (a) Although he was the last to cross the line, he completed the run.
  (b) Last but not the least, he called the meeting off unexpectedly.
  (c) Last year, I went to the much acclaimed food truck festival.
  (d) The last topic of the day is debate writing.

(3) exhausted (line 15)
  (a) With his fall, Owens had exhausted all of his chances at winning.
  (b) By the time I reached home, I was thoroughly exhausted.
  (c) You have exhausted the last of gas left to cook food.
  (d) Traditional burn farming methods have exhausted the soil.

(ii) Answer the following questions in your own words as briefly as possible.
  (a) What does the writer say about the size and movement of the sharks? (2)
  (b) Why was Teriakai chosen for special jobs? (2)
  (c) How did Teraikai ensure the safety of the captain and chief engineer? (2)

(iii) With close reference to the extract and in not more than 100 words, describe how the Gilbertese captured a tiger shark. (Failure to keep within the word limit will be penalised). (8)

Answers *in Topper's Style*

1. (i) I still remember the day vividly. It is the memory of that day that still causes deep embarrassment and is a source of joke for my friends. I was in middle school and it was the athletic meet. The stands were filled with parents and students. Sports had always been my passion and I was the fastest runner for the school. No surprise that I was beyond excited for the day and had prepared for it for weeks. When the time came for my race, I was nervous yet determined to win it. It was a relay race and my success also led to the success of my friends. The race started smoothly with everything going as planned and my team leading the race. I was the third player for my team and had to play a crucial role. As soon as the baton touched my fingers I ran as fast as my legs could. The wind was whipping my hair back and my eyes could clearly see the happy expressions of my fellow teammates cheering me on. Everything was perfect at that moment. It was when I was passing on the baton to my teammate that I fell flat on my face. It was later on I realised that my shoe laces had got tangled leading me to stumble and embarrass myself on one of the most important days of my school year.

There I was lying on the ground cheeks red with embarrassment but still a smile on my face because my team had won. It was to my stark relief that my teammate didn't stop and continued on leading us all to victory. From that day onwards, this became a funny story that deeply amuses my friends.

(ii) Today, I am going to share an interesting experience from my childhood. This experience is full of innocent courage that I obviously lack now. I was about 7 or 8 years old when I had to travel to Raiganj, a small town in West Bengal, to attend my uncle's wedding. Our ancestral house in the town was a big villa with a huge garden full of different plants. All of the children present in the house had already been cautioned to not go inside the garden as it was home to innumerable insects and animals which could harm us.

Taking care of the caution, we all assembled in the safe open verandah to play some games. While playing cricket there, my elder cousin hit the ball so hard that it went towards the nearby bushes. As I ran after the ball, I saw it disappear near a bush into the garden. I looked carefully and finally located it deep down in a ditch behind the bush. I thought I could reach it with my hands without going into the garden. Lying down on the ground, I stretched my hand as far as I could, slowly inching forward. I was just about reaching it, when to my horror, I fell into the ditch.

After I recovered from the shock I sat down to look at my injuries. My legs were scraped and my head was bleeding. I was in panic mode and had started crying when I realised that I had mistaken a hollow plastic shell, to be our ball. I screamed for help but to no avail. The scene inside the ditch was fearful with spiders and many other insects crawling around. My clothes were soiled and I was sweating badly. Dusk was fast approaching. The thought of spending the night in this well of misery terrified me. I made many attempts to get out but each time slipped back into the ditch.

All of a sudden, I heard the sound of a hiss. Fearing the worst, I decided not to move for I had heard that snakes bite when distracted. I gathered some courage and peeped down. My worst fears had come true.

There was big black snake behind me sitting quietly looking directly at my scraped leg. As he was inching near me, I took it by the tail and threw it at the big stone in the ditch.

Just then, I heard my brother calling out to me. I started shouting on top of my voice. Thankfully, he had located me as well as the snake. Hurriedly, he pulled me out of the ditch and called the elders to get rid of the snake. As I was weeping inconsolably, he comforted me and brought me home where my grandfather was informed that the snake had died and I was lucky to be safe as it was none other than the King Cobra.

(iii) **For the Motion**

In the present world, where we all are working towards sustainability, the concern of animal rights has become even more prevalent. With an increasing understanding of animal rights, people all across the globe are accepting and recognising the fact that animals are creatures with feelings, just like human beings. Thus, just like us, the animals around us also deserve safety and security. Therefore, I believe that the decision of the government to ban the dissection of animals in laboratories is justified.

It is not strange to state that most of the houses today have pets at home. We love them and care for them just like family. These pets reciprocate our feelings. Think about it. Do they not respond to feelings of affection or even when they are reprimanded for some wrong action on their part? We all know the answer to this question. Animals do show their emotions. They also feel pain, happiness, guilt, etc. Then, why do we want to kill and abuse animals for no fault of theirs?

Many would point that science does not have any other option as experiments needs to be performed on living beings for furthering the cause of research or as a part of essential biological or medical education. Well, this research can be carried out by other means too like by using modern technology and without dissecting animals. What use is modern technology if we do not apply it in different fields?

Further, a demonstration, which I believe is the major reason for such experimentation, can even be shown by providing models of suitable cross-sections of the insides of the animals to be studied. Such models can be made by commercial organisations for sale to educational institutions. This will also prevent repetition of such killings and dissections in future which promote education and research.

In addition, we cannot forget the ecological imbalance caused by such senseless killing of animals. In this light, the government's decision works well as it also functions to maintain the ecological balance and biodiversity all the while promoting environment preservation and conservation.

The relentless killing of animals is inhumane as well as unethical. Hence, it is my earnest appeal to ban the use of animals in laboratories for the purpose of dissection.

Against the Motion

The very first understanding of science and biology came to be with dissection. Since the first discovery of organs and biological mechanisms, dissection of animals had been central to the understanding of biological processes and, thus, institutions have been using it for teaching and education purposes. The purpose behind dissection is simple. It provides a practical experience of the theoretical knowledge that students learn from books. They get an opportunity to actually put their learning to practice.

The dissection of animals has a scientific purpose; it is a mode of hands-on education for students wherein they actually look at what they are being taught. Looking at this act of education as unjust is flawed because its sole purpose is meant to develop a student's knowledge of the elements and functions of the living being. Now, there might've been other ways to do so through models. However, I would like to point that even then, the real time understanding will be lost. The purpose of dissection will be lost as the entire process will become similar to theoretical knowledge which I feel is not enough for a science or biology related subjects.

Further, we should give more credit to the sensitivity and intelligence of authorities as well as students so as not to believe that a dissection class will make them more prone to animal violence. Students understand the value of animal life and how an animal has the same kind of organs as human beings. The governing philosophy behind teaching students to dissect animals should be that life, whether human or animal, is the same; all living beings are tied to one other by their inner similarity. With this ideology, all dissections are performed with the view of keeping the animals alive. Proper methods are used by institutions to make sure that animals that are a part of dissections or experiments are properly tended and kept alive.

Thus, a ban on dissection of animals in laboratories would not be the best course of action.

(iv) **Dreams**

'The future belongs to those who dream and believe in the beauty of dreams.'

Dreams can be defined simply as a series of thoughts, visions or feelings we imagine while we are asleep. A very simple occurring event which is often emblematic of a sound sleep, dreams have been a subject of research for many people since long. Consequently, there are many aspects of dreams that have remained unearthed. Philosophically, dreams are often understood by psychologists as the manifestation of what we want to achieve, what we aspire to become and how we want to live. Dreams are then essential because they keep us motivated. At night, when we dream, we often think about what we want to achieve in life. We imagine the situation in vivid details including how was the scenario and how we will feel when we achieve our dream. The sheer visualisation of our goals, aims and desires, encourage us to move ahead in life and work hard to achieve it.

There are many examples of people who have dreamt and had worked for it to finally achieve it. Be it the king of Bollywood, Shah Rukh Khan or the King of Cricket, Sachin Tendulkar, all of the successful people that we have heard of did not achieve success without a goal. All of them had a goal and had dreamt of achieving that goal. Dreams gave purpose to their lives. In this light, a person who does not dream has no sense of life. Such a person is like an aimless wanderer who is living just for the sake of living. Dreams then are a royal road to understanding the self.

Another understanding of dreams is that they are a means of escaping the stress and worries of life. The modern world fills man with monotony, stress, anxiety and pessimism. In such cases, dreams take a creative and a highly imaginative path. We imagine the existence of things that do not exist in reality. We imagine travelling back to history, meeting an idol and all of the things that are practically impossible to achieve in the real world.

While it is very difficult for anyone to objectively understand, define and characterise dreams, it is crucial to point out that they are natural to all human beings. They are the reality like manifestation of our feelings that can be as beautiful as a peaceful snow-covered mountain and as scary and terrifying as a horror movie. They are mystic, mysterious and inexplicable while being motivating, aspiring and encouraging.

(v) Human beings, by their inherent nature, are social beings. They need to communicate their feelings, ideas and thoughts to live amongst their own kind and by default find that words are the means to do so. They forget that words are merely sounds uttered by the tongue. It is actually the actions that put the meaning into the said words. The age old proverb 'Action speaks louder than words' is central to man's social position as it depicts this importance of actions over words.

Banking upon the boastful nature of people that one can encounter in life, the proverb highlights that there is no need to just say some words when your actions can very well speak for you. Words, then, are just excuses to hide a lack of determination. Determined people never speak or boast about themselves. Their performance and actions have more voice than their words.

An individual is made up of his/her actions. It determines an individual's personality, strength of character and desire to progress. What someone does and how that person behaves in a particular situation reveals the true nature of that person. If a person merely speaks about his/her achievements, he/she is often regarded as a boastful individual. Such an individual is most often seen in a negative light as an untrustworthy individual.

Merely speaking then comes out as a futile task as words can be easily manipulated to fit in a given situation. By using words, it becomes very easy for one to define oneself in a way that appeals to everybody and make promises that would never be fulfilled. A person may have several plans but they are worthless until culminated in actions.

People who just speak of their plans show self-importance, pride and arrogance don't actually achieve anything. People who want to be successful in life work hard towards their goals. Such people come out of their comfort zones and take appropriate actions for their progress. Their actions and achievements speak for themselves. People get to know about it without any mention. Hard working students never speak much about their success, rather they keep working with determination to achieve that success. Later, it is their grades that speak for them. Similarly, a leader who chooses action rather than words can take a nation towards success.

Concluding, ego and self-praise can reduce the worth of an achievement. The history of mankind has seen that down-to-earth people who believe in action have always been successful. All one needs to do is follow one's dreams, perform with dedication and soon one's actions will definitely speak louder than words.

(vi) I knew at once that the blue envelope was from her. My hands trembled as I reached for it. This was the 5th envelope I had received from her in the past month. All communication arrived through various mediums. The first letter was hidden inside my Sunday Times just under my gate. I opened it as I was curious to know the content. I received the information to keep myself free on 28th December. All communications used the same stationary, same stack of envelopes and same coloured ink. Through different sources I had received five envelopes informing the same matter to keep myself free on 28th December.

I remember the date very well. This was the day an important event had happened which annoyed my parents. Who was this lady who wanted to meet me and why? Let me tell you the event which had occurred on 28th December, 2011. My parents wanted me to get married. They had arranged a meeting with a girl whose family was of their choice. I was dating some other girl but did not have the courage to tell the truth to my parents.

Evening came and we went to meet the family and the girl. Everything was fine and the girl and myself were left alone to spend some time with each other.

The girl started crying as soon as she was left alone with me. She told me that she loved somebody else but could not tell this truth to her parents. She asked me to do a favour to her. She requested that I should say 'no' for her in front of her parents. As I myself was not interested in marrying her, so I said no in front of her parents. She cried to show everybody that she was quite disturbed.

When we came back, my father was quite annoyed with me. Many years have passed since then and I had moved on in my life. Now, I was receiving letters from her to keep myself free on that day. Anyway, I remained anxious till that day. It was a suspense which I was not able to solve. I did not share this with anyone. Finally, the much awaited day arrived. As instructed, I reached the B-36 Bungalow on Shivaji road exactly at 5:30 pm. I pressed the bell with a fast beating heart. The lady opened the door with a smiling face. Looking at her face, I immediately recognised her face but still I was anxious why she had called me. She asked me to sit and relax. She told me that she was very happy and she wanted to convey her thanks by meeting me personally. When I asked her how she knew my address or number, she called her husband. Looking at him, I was surprised and shocked as he was nobody else, but a distant cousin of mine with whom I had not been in touch for a long time!

It was really a pleasant surprise that the girl who refused to marry me was married to one of my relatives and it was because of me she was really happy. It was like a dream come true for me.

2. (i) **Indian Population Explosion : A Grave Challenge**

by Srishti Chauhan

India is the most populated country in the world, and it is sufficient to say that its population bomb is ticking. In our country, a baby is born every two seconds, i.e. more than 40,000 children are born every day. If the present trend continues, our population will touch the scary figure of a thousand million soon.

The evil effects of over-population are too obvious to need any explanation. It is one of the root causes of many of the socio-economic crisis the nation is facing today. The very first problem it brings is the lack of resources. It is not hidden from anyone that the limited resources of our planet are already getting relinquished and their renewal will take thousands of years. In this light, we are still cutting trees, reducing forest areas and exploiting water bodies to accustom the ever increasing population of the nation. This puts immense pressure on nature which becomes prone to climatic changes and disasters.

Further, the unbridled growth of human population has also brought problems like unemployment, urbanisation, pollution, etc. neutralising all kinds of economic growth and development. One may wonder what is the cause of such population rise. The answer is illiteracy and lack of awareness about what overpopulation is doing to our nation and the world at large.

Hence, it is necessary that the problem of population growth is attacked on a war-footing. The masses have to be motivated and not coerced to adopt family planning. And the best method to motivate is to educate. Television can play a very useful role in this regard. We should not spare any attempt to educate our people and convince them of the benefits-both social and individual-about a controlled growth of population.

Many people have virtually given up hope. They may be right but, if we lose hope, then any chance of succeeding against this bomb will be lost. We need not only a renewal of interest in population control but also a renewal of faith in ourselves, in our cultural heritage and in the capacity of democracy in making the population an asset.

(ii) **Proposal for Setting up a Physics Club**

Heading/Introduction To foster an interest in Physics outside the classroom and introduce students to the wonders and relevance of learning the concepts of physics as a subject in our lives, we propose to set up a Physics Club in school.

Objectives A Physics Club will help students overcome their phobias regarding the specific field of Science. It will be instrumental in developing the scientific curiosity of students through its activities and programmes.

List of Measures

- The Physics Laboratory of the school will be used as the room for all the club meetings and activities.
- The meetings will take place twice a week after school from 2:00 pm till 3:30 pm. Any activities such as talks by scientists or competitions will take place on Saturdays.
- Membership of the club will be open to all students from Classes VI to XII. The Club President will be Mr. Singhania, our Senior Physics Teacher. Eight other office bearers will be elected from among the members of the club.

- Club membership has been fixed at ₹ 400/- per member per year.
- The club will have a range of activities ranging from Science fairs, robot making workshops and competitions, quizzes, etc. that boost scientific curiosity.

We hope that the proposal will be accepted so that the Science Club becomes a reality in the school.

3. (i) (a) Despite it being a cloudy day, the temperature was 45°C.

(b) The entire block of flats is being demolished by them.

(c) Anil was of the opinion that the examination would be held later.

(d) You like this food more than I do.

(e) In spite of failing in the examination, Raju was not upset.

(ii)

(a) to	(b) against	(c) away	(d) by
(e) from	(f) on	(g) up	(h) down
(i) for	(j) over		

(iii)

1. struck	2. burning	3. drawn	4. keeps
5. burning	6. bathed	7. caught	8. moved
9. glanced	10. went		

4. (i) (a) (1) brute (2) grimly (3) welter

(b) (1) (a) The Lions Club distributed blankets to the poor on the new year eve.

(2) (c) Last year, I went to the much acclaimed food truck festival.

(3) (b) By the time I reached home, I was thoroughly exhausted.

(ii) (a) In the given passage, the author mentions that the sharks vary in size ranging from nine to fourteen feet in length. They can occasionally be as big as eighteen feet. The author also mentions that the sharks move with a slack grace. They slide and swoop easily and gracefully but their movements are rather slow.

(b) Teriakai was always chosen for hard and special jobs because his strong, stout body and strength matched well with the giant-like strength of the shark.

(c) Teriakai ensured the safety of the captain and chief engineer by making him stay inside a fine bag made out of the mainsail while he himself set out to the shore to seek help.

(iii) To capture a tiger shark, the Gilbertese sailed in a small canoe with a line fastened to it. When a tiger shark took the hook, the boat used to tilt suddenly. With the shark, the canoe whirled around, sinking or rising madly at times while the fisherman held onto his line relentlessly. After some time, the tiger shark would be exhausted and would stop struggling. The dead body of the tiger shark would, then, float on the surface of the water which would be taken by the fisherman.

SQP Code : **PB-8/10** Series ***i*-Succeed 8-25/10** Roll No. | | | | | | | | |

Sample Question Paper 08

English Language 12th (Code 801)

General Instructions

1. You are allowed additional 15 minutes for only reading the question paper.
2. You must NOT start writing during reading time.
3. It has four questions in all.
4. Answer all questions.
5. You are advised to spend not more than 45 minutes on Question 1, 55 minutes on Question 2, 30 minutes on Question 3 and 50 minutes on Question 4.
6. You should begin each answer on a fresh page.
7. The intended marks for questions are given in brackets [ ].

Time : 3 Hrs.
Max. Marks : 80

Question 1.

Write a composition (in approximately 400-450 words) on any one of the following subjects. (20)

(You are reminded that you will be rewarded for orderly and coherent presentation of material, use of appropriate style and general accuracy of spelling, punctuation and grammar.)

(i) The sounds of laughter and loud voices attract your attention to a room in your house. The door is closed. Describe what you hear or what you see as you gently open the door.

(ii) Narrate an incident from your own experiences when you prepared a meal. Explain what you did and what you gained from the experience.

(iii) "Private cars should be banned in the congested commercial areas of the cities." Write for or against the topic.

(iv) Inspiration

(v) "Elements of Western culture have had a very influential role on cultures of the world." Express your views on the statement.

(vi) Write an original short story which illustrates the truth of the statement 'One lie leads to another'.

Question 2.

(i) Write a review of any book that you have read recently in about 300 words. (15)

Hints

Title of the book- author- main characters- story in brief- critical evaluation- discuss story writing, plot, character development, etc- overall opinion- rating.

(ii) As the Head Boy/Head Girl of your school, you have been given the responsibility of organising an excursion for the students of Classes XI and XII to Ranthambore National Park. Write a proposal in about 150 words stating the steps you would take to successfully organise the excursion. (10)

Question 3.

Answer sections **(i)**, **(ii)** and **(iii)**

(i) Rewrite the following sentences according to the instructions given after each of them in the brackets.

(a) If he does not run fast, he will lose the race.
Use: (Unless ....will..............)

(b) I do not like this food as much as you do.
Use: (......more...........)

(c) On seeing the rat, she shrieked.
Begin: (As soon as ....)

(d) You must never tell a lie.
Begin: (Under no circumstances...............)

(e) The boss said, "What an extraordinary success!"
Begin: (The boss exclaimed ....)

(ii) In the following sentences, replace the **INCORRECT** underlined words to make the sentences more meaningful and grammatically correct. (Do not copy the sentence) (5)

(a) If we set <u>for</u> early, we can return before sunset.

(b) He left the company for good and set <u>down</u> his own business.

(c) The teacher jumped <u>over</u> a conclusion and punished the child.

(d) Ramesh jumped <u>at</u> my offer of a job.

(e) I am a simple man and have no use <u>of</u> much money.

(f) My father lost the use <u>for</u> his right arm in an accident.

(g) Rahul decided to carry <u>over</u> with tennis.

(h) Dinanath is a good worker and is always ready to carry <u>after</u> his masters orders.

SP-08

(i) Reena agreed <u>by</u> me when I proposed a meeting.

(j) The four sisters couldn't agree <u>with</u> themselves.

(iii) Fill in the blanks in the passage given below with the appropriate form of the verb given in brackets. Do not write the passage but write the verbs in correct order. (5)

The other day we .... **(1)** (discuss) the setting up of a Debating Club in our school. We ...... **(2)** (talk) about the club and how many students ...... **(3)** (be) interested in it. Then, we ...... **(4)** (begin) to talk about the rules and regulations that .... **(5)** (govern) the club. None of us could ...... **(6)** (agree) and we began ...... **(7)** (argue). Finally, our English teacher ... **(8)** (have) to be informed and she .... **(9)** (come) and .... **(10)** (break) up the meeting.

Question 4.

Read the passage given below and answer the questions (i), (ii) and (iii) that follow.

The Hidden Box

(1) I opened the iron gate and walked as softly as I could up the weed-tufted gravel drive. My mind was strangely empty. I felt no glow of pleasure and was unexcited at the prospect of becoming rich. I was occupied only with the mechanical task of **finding** a black box.

(2) The front door was closed and set far back in a very deep porch. The wind and rain had whipped a coating of gritty dust against the panels, showing that it had been shut for years.

Standing on a derelict flower-bed, I tried to push open the first window on the left. It yielded to my strength stubbornly. I clambered through the opening and found myself crawling along the deepest window-ledge I had ever seen. After I had jumped noisily down upon the floor, I looked up.

(3) The room was thick with dust, musty and empty of all furniture. Spiders had erected great stretchings of their webs about the fireplace. I made my way quickly to the room where the box was and paused on the threshold. It was a dark morning and the weather had stained the windows with blears of grey wash which kept the brightest part of the weak fight from coming in. The far corner of the room was a blur of shadow. I had a sudden impulse to have done with my task and be out of this house forever.

I walked across the bare boards, knelt down in the corner and passed my hands about the floor in search of the lose board. To my surprise, I found it easily. I lifted it up, laid it aside' and struck a match. I saw a black metal cash-box nestling dimly in the hole. I put my hand down and crooked a finger into the loose reclining **handle**, but the match suddenly flickered and went out and the handle of the box, which I had lifted up about an inch, slide heavily off my finger. Without stopping to light another match, I **thrust** my hand into the opening and just when it should be closing about the box, something happened.

(4) I cannot hope to describe what it was but it had frightened me very much. It was some change which came upon me or upon the room, indescribably subtle, yet momentous. It was as if the daylight had changed with unnatural suddenness, as if the temperature had altered greatly in an instant or as if the air had become twice as rare or twice as dense as it had been in the twinkling of an eye. Perhaps all of these or other things, happened together, for all my senses were bewildered all at once and could give me no explanation. The fingers of my right hand, thrust in the opening in the floor, had closed mechanically, found nothing at all and came up again empty. The box had gone!

(5) I heard a cough behind me, soft and natural, yet more disturbing than any sound that could ever come upon the human ear. That I did not die of fright was due, I think, to two things: the fact that my senses were already disarranged and able to interpret to me only gradually what they had perceived and also the fact that the utterance of the cough seemed to bring with it some more awful alteration in everything. I collapsed weakly into a limp sitting-down position upon the floor.

Sweat broke out on my brow and my eyes remained open for a long time without a wink..

(6) In the darkest corner of the room near the window, a man was sitting in a chair, eyeing me with a mild but unwavering interest.

(i) (a) Find a single word from the passage that will exactly replace the underlined word or words in the following sentences. (3)

(1) There is hardly any <u>likelihood</u> of him failing his examintaion after preparing for it for a year.

(2) The cow sat at the <u>shelter in front of the entrance</u> of their house.

(3) She was left <u>confused</u> after his reaction on seeing her secure first position in the dance competition.

(b) For each of the words given below, choose the correct sentence that uses the same word unchanged in spelling, but with a different meaning from that it carries in the passage. (3)

(1) finding (line 3)

(a) I'm fed up with constantly finding you in the hallway sifting through the letters.

(b) The committee has submitted its finding on the origin of the sacrificial ritual.

(c) He was finding it increasingly difficult to make decisions.

(d) She dreads her husband finding out about the unnecessary shopping.

SP-08

(2) handle (line 20)
  (a) You won't be able to handle this job.
  (b) Don't take on more than you can handle.
  (c) Please handle this precision instrument carefully.
  (d) All of the above

(3) thrust (line 22)
  (a) She tried to thrust back the little stabs of home - sickness.
  (b) With an impatient gesture he thrust the food away from him.
  (c) He hunched his shoulders and thrust his hands deep into his pockets.
  (d) All of the above

(ii) Answer the following questions in your own words as briefly as possible.
  (a) What details show that the house had been shut for years? (2)
  (b) Why did the narrator have a feeling of uneasiness and fear when he entered the room? (2)
  (c) What was the strange thing that happened about the box? What impact did it have on the narrator? (2)

(iii) Describe the narrator's purpose behind entering the abandoned house and the strange atmosphere he encountered there in not more than 100 words. (8)

Answers *in Topper's Style*

1. (i) It was a peaceful summer night and also my birthday eve. Summer vacations were going on and I had expected my friends to be enjoying their vacations. Hence, it was a usual night for me. All was quiet except the noise of ACs and coolers. I was sleeping soundly dreaming of some exotic places and travelling in a fast moving train. Suddenly, the AC began to make too much sound. I was sleepy and confused at the same time. Why would the AC make such strange sounds? As I was wondering about it, the silence of the night was filled with a loud laughter and giggling.

I woke up with a start. My confusion increased when I realised that the sounds did not stop. In fact, as I listened closely, I found that it was coming from somewhere inside my house. I got up scared and wondered where the sounds were coming from as my parents were away to their hometown and my grandparents would be sleeping soundly by now. There were many questions which were troubling my mind and I decided to check.

I tiptoed and followed the direction of the sound. I could hear a distinct sound of laughter, giggling and human sound talking excitedly from the hall. This made me curious and I wanted to open the door to the hall. My curiosity got the better of me and I pushed open the door. The room was in total darkness and the sound stopped. All I could hear was ticking of the wall clock. Where were all the people who were making those sounds? Why had those sounds stopped? Surely, everyone could not disappear in a flash.

Now I was terrified of what I might encounter. However, I gathered all courage and took a step inside. I moved further inside and stood upon the side of a bed trying to switch on the light. From my peripheral vision, I could see some vague shapes on one side of the room. Somehow, I switched on the light hoping that everything would be fine.

As soon as I switched on the lights, I heard lively music and saw lots of figures coming out of their hiding places. I had frozen at the spot and only relaxed when I saw that those figures were none other than my parents, my siblings and some of my friends. They all began to sing 'Happy Birthday to you'. I was surprised to say the least as I had not expected such a grand gesture. They had planned a surprise birthday party in the honour of 'Sleeping Beauty', *i.e.* me.

(ii) I still remember the day when I prepared the first meal all by myself. It was a winter evening and my family was out for some shopping. I had just returned from my tuitions and was famished. There was nothing healthy for me to eat. So, I decided to cook an omelette for myself. I had seen my mother do it plenty of times and felt that I could also do it. After all, how difficult could it be.

I decided to prepare my ingredients first. I took two eggs, one tomato and a large onion. I chopped the onion on the chopping board just as I had seen chefs do it. Then, came the tomatoes. I washed it and started chopping. It definitely was a daunting task. I had even slashed my skin at many places. Fortunately, there was no bleeding only a slight burning in those cuts.

After the chopping was done, I decided to whip the eggs. It took me two to three attempts to crack open the eggs and drop them into the whipping bowl. The spices were next. My mother always kept the spices on the top shelf in the kitchen. I couldn't reach them, so I got a stool and got the chilli powder and salt. I put all the ingredients in a bowl with the eggs and whisked them. I lit the stove, put the big frying pan on it and poured some oil in the pan.

After the oil had heated, I poured the batter into the pan. Everything was going perfect when I was struck with a thought. How would I flip my omelette! I decided to use a spoon but my attempt failed. Soon, I was running all over the kitchen, searching all the shelves and drawers to find the flat cooking spoon; all the while, the omelet was sizzling in the pan.

Finally, I found the spoon and made a rush to turn over the omelette. I managed to do that without breaking or spilling it out of the pan, only to see a very nicely cooked side up.

While I was busy taking it out in a plate, someone came up behind me. It was mom; she was angry and dumbstruck. The kitchen was in a mess, with the drawers all open and some salt and chilli powder on the stove and countertop. She was also shocked at my successful attempt at making an omelette. She, then, helped me clean the kitchen and also promised to teach me at least some simple dishes.

(iii) **For the Motion**

'Toxic Smog: Fear for health, the malady of pollution, smog transcends over the region...' these are some of the common news reports that we hear on a daily basis. Pollution has always been a central problem we face in our lives but now it has become so prominent that if we do not do something about it, survival on Earth would become difficult. One might wonder what is causing pollution even when the government and the people are becoming aware and also taking steps to reduce it.

We can easily find the answer to this question every day, out in the streets with hundreds of vehicles running along the roads. Numerous studies have shown that vehicular pollution is on the rise and so is the traffic. Today, every individual owns a car and uses it to travel anywhere without any thought or rather ignoring how it can be detrimental to everyone. More and more cars means more pollution and many other problems including less parking space, more accidents, more congestion, etc. While the use of cars cannot be stopped or reduced drastically as it is a transport of convenience, it can be banned in the congested commercial areas of cities.

The advantages of implementing the ban will be many. First, it will lead to less congestion, less problem for pedestrians and no road rage incidents. Second, less vehicles would mean less exhaust emission and less time wasted on roads which in turn will increase the efficiency of people. Let my opponents not forget that banning cars in the congested areas will also reduce noise pollution which has reached alarming levels and has become a major woe for many stratums of the society. Further, it will function to create more space for safe movement of all and the vehicles carrying goods in the commercial hubs and emergency services will carry on with more ease thereby saving time too.

To conclude, this step should be taken at the earliest as it will immensely benefit the people of the commercial areas and become a path-breaking example for others to follow suit.

Against the Motion

While I am in favour of taking steps to solve the problem of pollution, parking space, accidents and more congestion, I am not in favour of a banning of private cars from entering congested commercial areas for various reasons.

We all know that having a private car allows an individual to travel to all places in comfort. Hence, many people rely heavily on their cars for travel. If they were to stop the use of private cars, they would not have a good and efficient suitable alternative to do so. One might say that there is public transport but all of us know that our public transport system is not efficient enough to satisfy the needs of travel for the entire population or even the majority of people living in cities. Further, freedom of travelling is inhibited when one is at the mercy of public vehicles. It has its scheduled places and time of departures and stops.

Moreover, if traders and their customers use taxis or autos, it will become a very costly affair. Therefore, trade and business will suffer as there will be an increase in travel expenditure. This will further lead to an increase in the retail price of commodities which will cause more difficulties for the common man. Thus, both business and the economy will be adversely affected due to such a measure and this is something that we cannot afford. In addition, this action will not reduce the level of congestion itself as the surrounding areas may get heavily congested.

So, government should think over some other strategy to overcome the problem of pollution like odd-even rule, which was tried earlier with limited success. Further, the solution must involve looking at the real cause of congestion including the maintenance of roads, movement of commercial vehicles, lack of traffic signals and so on. One can also not forget that public transport can be made more efficient for the same.

Thus, pollution can be contained without putting a ban on cars in congested commercial areas.

(iv) **Inspiration**

"When your Daemon is in charge, do not try to think consciously. Drift, wait and obey." - Rudyard Kipling

In a culture obsessed with measuring talent and ability, we often overlook the important role of inspiration in defining our goals and leading us on the path to success. Inspiration is that aspect of life that awakens us to new possibilities by allowing us to transcend our ordinary experiences and limitations. It brings opportunities that help us challenge our notions and constraints. It propels a person to possibility and transforms the way we perceive our own capabilities. It may be overlooked but it always exists in some form or the other- be it a near and dear one or a popular person like a celebrity, a freedom fighter, etc.

We get inspired by something or by various individuals in our day-to-day existence. When we notice some great characteristics in others, we feel the urge to inculcate that characteristic in our life. It adjusts our point of view of living and makes us think positively. Having an inspiration has an incredible effect on our considerations and assists us with accomplishing our objectives and getting achievement.

Inspired people are more open to new experiences and always accept whatever knowledge comes in their way. Additionally, they believe that inspiration is something that happens to you spontaneously and is not willed. Inspired individuals also have a stronger drive to master their work and are less competitive. They are more intrinsically motivated as they have higher levels of important psychological resources including belief in their own abilities, self-esteem and optimism.

Further, it can be said that inspiration is the springboard for creativity. Inspired people view themselves as more creative and are often found to be great artists. Being in a state of inspiration also predicts the creativity of writing samples across scientific writing, poetry and fiction. Inspired writers are more efficient and productive and spend less time pausing and more time writing. Inspiration facilitates progress toward goals. People who were generally more inspired in their daily lives also tend to set inspired goals, which were more likely to be successfully attained.

This does not mean that inspiration is completely outside your control. Contrary to the view of inspiration being purely mythical or divine, I think inspiration is best thought of as a surprising interaction between your current knowledge and the information you receive from the world.

To become personally inspired, the best you can do is set up the optimal circumstances for inspiration. As a society, the best we can do is assist in setting up these important circumstances for everyone. An easy first step is simply recognising the sheer potency of inspiration and its potential impact on everything we do.

(v) It is not uncommon for all of us to hear about the increasing impact of the Western culture on the native cultures of different regions across the globe. The rapid colonisation of different parts of the world by the European powers in the last two centuries had pioneered a shift from a traditional native culture to a westernised version of the same culture. Our nation had itself undergone a substantial westernisation to such an extent that today many traditional cultural forms are lost to Indians.

While we cannot talk about a generic effect of Western culture on different cultures, we can talk about how it had impacted India- the land of innumerable cultural diversities. The Indian culture is basically family-oriented which contrasts with the individual-oriented approach of the Western culture. Westernisation had, then, resulted in the creation of nuclear families with fewer kinship ties. It is, thus, common to find many youngsters moving out of their parent's home to stay on their own.

Besides being more individualistic, Western culture is also self-centered and gives a lot of importance to wealth, power and success. This materialistic orientation of western culture makes it more flexible and practical. Indian culture and society being more spiritual in nature, gives more importance to customs, traditions and family values. The impact of westernisation is visible here also as the younger generation does not want to participate in and in many cases even criticises many traditions.

Westernisation had made Indians selfish, individualistic and critical of the Indian cultural system all the while changing their lifestyle, clothing and even food habits. However, this is not to suggest that there is nothing good in Western culture. There are many important issues like gender equality, human rights, progressive outlook to life and a spirit of competition which we are adopting from the West. This will make our life more meaningful and also develop the society and the nation.

The impact of westernisation may be very prevalent but this does not change the fact that even with Western ideals, our culture offers a unique example of 'Unity in Diversity' to the world. The customs enrich our lives, making the individual and the society more pleasant and peaceful. It is indeed a paradox that while we are adopting Western lifestyle, the people in the West are looking up to India for peace and salvation. They flock to India in search of peace, through meditation and yoga.

Agreeably, Western culture is versatile and has taught us to be progressive and self dependent. However, at the same time, it is more materialistic and individualistic in nature. Hence, we should not blindly adopt it. There is need to imbibe the good things from them without forgetting our culture and values, which makes us unique in the world.

(vi) **One Lie Leads to Another**

Saira was a sixteen-year-old girl belonging to a middle class family. She went to a really expensive private school as she was smart in academics. She was friends with many rich students but her best friend was Anna. Anna was good at studies too but she was also interested in other things. Besides studies, she talked to Saira about fashion, jewellery, concerts and parties, etc. Although Saira was not really interested in these things before, hearing about them made her want to do all the things that Anna did. One day, Anna told her that she was going to The Towers with some friends and asked her to join them. Saira knew that her parents would never allow her to go with Anna but she really wanted to have fun so she decided to go with them.

Next day, Saira told her mother that she would be late from school as there was an extra class and took some money from her large college savings. She felt uneasy about lying to her parents but forgot all about it soon. When her parents asked her about the extra class, she again lied that she had been working on a project with her science teacher.

After some days, Anna again asked her to join them and Saira agreed. This became a routine and Saira's excuses continued. As a result, her studies were affected while her college savings reduced.

One day, when Saira's mother was cleaning her cupboard, she noticed that the money Saira had saved for college had reduced significantly. When she asked Saira about it, the latter got afraid. She did not want her mother to find out that she goes out with Anna. So, she lied and said she did not know about it.

Her mother started scolding their maid thinking that she was the culprit. The maid was terrified and started crying, which made Saira feel guilty. She was frightened but she also wanted to save the innocent maid so she decided to lie yet again. She told her mother that she had taken the money to buy some books. Her mother was surprised and doubtful. So, she asked Saira to show her the books but Saira couldn't.

Finally realising that she could not escape the situation, Saira told her mother everything. Her mother was angry and scolded Saira. She decided to take the rest of the saved money so that Saira could not spend it recklessly. She also told Saira that she wasn't allowed to stay back in school until her teacher informs her of the same. Saira realised that her one lie led to so many other lies that she had lost the trust that her mother reposed in her. She promised that she would never lie again and apologised to her mother.

2. (i) Last weekend, I found myself in the mood for reading something ghostly. My elder sister suggested that I should read Oscar Wilde's 'The Canterville Ghost' because not only is it a horror story but it flips the script on the traditional ghost story by turning it into a witty and delightful romp. Set in a gloomy English manor, Canterville Chase, the tale revolves around Sir Simon, a weary ghost who's haunted the halls for centuries. However, his attempts to terrify the new American residents, the Otis family, fall hilariously flat. The Otises, with their pragmatic American spirit, are unfased by Sir Simon's theatrics. Mr. Otis offers him a ghost-removal guarantee, while the twins pelt him with pillows. Only Virginia, the kind-hearted daughter, shows any empathy for the frustrated ghost.

Wilde's sharp wit shines through in his portrayal of the clash between cultures. The stoic British ghost and the boisterous American family create a comedic goldmine. Sir Simon's despair at his failing haunting attempts is a constant source of amusement. While the story is undeniably funny, it also possesses a touch of melancholy. We learn of Sir Simon's tragic past, revealing the reason behind his restless spirit. This adds depth to the narrative and allows the reader to develop a grudging sympathy for the hapless ghost.

'The Canterville Ghost' is a charming novella, perfect for those seeking a light and entertaining read and I deeply enjoyed the experience of reading it. With its clever humor, memorable characters and surprising twists, it's a timeless classic that will leave you chuckling long after the final page.

(ii) **Proposal for Organising an Excursion to Ranthambore National Park**

Heading To foster students' interest in wildlife and to introduce them to the wonders of animals' life and living, we propose to organise an excursion.

Objectives The excursion to the National Park will be both enjoyable and enriching leaving some useful learning behind with the students. The students will develop a love for wildlife.

List of measures

- To arrange buses for the trip.
- To make an arrangement for rooms or dormitories to accommodate the students.
- To organise fun activities to keep the trip energetic and enthusiastic.
- The students will be accompanied by History and Geography teachers Mr. Arun, Ms Asha and Ms Sumita for better understanding of wildlife.
- The trip will cost ₹ 1500 per person and will include transport, lodging and food charges.

We hope that this proposal will be accepted so that the excursion will be arranged as soon as possible.

3. (i) (a) Unless he runs fast, he will lose the race.
(b) You like this food more than I do.
(c) As soon as she saw the rat, she shrieked.
(d) Under no circumstances must you tell a lie.
(e) The boss exclaimed with joy that it was an extraordinary success.

(ii)

(a) out	(b) up	(c) to	(d) at
(e) for	(f) of	(g) on	(h) out
(i) with	(j) among		

(iii)

1. were discussing	2. talked	3. were	4. began
5. would govern	6. agree	7. arguing	8. had
9. came	10. broke		

4. (i) (a) (1) prospect
(2) porch
(3) bewildered

(b) (1) (b) The committee has submitted its finding on the origin of the sacrificial rituals.
(2) (d) All of the above
(3) (d) All of the above

(ii) (a) The wind and rain had whipped a coating of gritty dust against the panels. The room inside was thick with dust, musty and empty of all furniture and the spiders had erected great stretchings of their webs about the fireplace. All these things show that the house had been shut for years.

(b) The narrator had a feeling of uneasiness and fear when he entered the room because the room was thick with dust, musty and empty of all furniture. He thrust his hand into the opening and just when it should be closing about the box something happened.

(c) When the narrator saw the box, he put his hand down and crooked a finger into the loose reclining handle of the box, he had lifted it about an inch but the match suddenly flickered and the box slid heavily off his finger. When he again put his hand near the box, something unnatural happened.
After this, the narrator became very frightened.

(iii) The narrator's purpose of entering the house was to find the black hidden box. He was not excited at the prospect of becoming rich but he had to find the box. He reached the location and found the black box inside the hole. It slid off his finger and again when he put his hand near the box. As soon as he did so, a change came in the environment. The daylight had changed with unnatural suddenness, the temperature had altered greatly or the air had become twice as rare or twice as dense as it had been in the twinkling of the eye.

SQP Code : **PB-9/10** Series ***i*-Succeed 9-25/10** Roll No. | | | | | | | | |

Sample Question Paper 09

English Language 12th (Code 801)

General Instructions

1. You are allowed additional 15 minutes for only reading the question paper.
2. You must NOT start writing during reading time.
3. It has four questions in all.
4. Answer all questions.
5. You are advised to spend not more than 45 minutes on Question 1, 55 minutes on Question 2, 30 minutes on Question 3 and 50 minutes on Question 4.
6. You should begin each answer on a fresh page.
7. The intended marks for questions are given in brackets [ ].

Time : 3 Hrs.

Max. Marks : 80

Question 1.

Write a composition (in approximately 400-450 words) on any one of the following subjects. (20)

(You are reminded that you will be rewarded for orderly and coherent presentation of material, use of appropriate style and general accuracy of spelling, punctuation and grammar.)

(i) Recently, you had travelled by bus. Describe your experience of visit to the bus stand.

(ii) Your father is an avid traveller and loves to seek new experiences. Narrate your experiences of one special trip that you took along with your father.

(iii) "Admission to top-notch institutes guarantees a successful career." Write **for** or **against** the motion.

(iv) Superstition

(v) 'Experience is the best teacher.' Express your views on the statement.

(vi) Write a short story titled 'The Box of Memories'.

Question 2.

(i) Write a newspaper report on the issue of potholes in your local area detailing their impact on daily life, the efforts being made by local authorities to address the problem, and the responses from the community. (15)

(ii) As the Head of the Student Council of your school, you have been assigned the responsibility of setting up a Culinary Club in your school. Write a proposal in about 150 words stating the steps you would take to establish this club. (10)

Question 3.

Answer sections **(i)**, **(ii)** and **(iii)**

(i) Rewrite the following sentences according to the instructions given after each of them in the brackets. (5)

(a) Ashita is the most beautiful girl in the class.
Begin: (No ....)

(b) As soon as she reached home, she learnt that she had to leave for London.
Use: (Hardly ....when.....................)

(c) Ramesh said , "Rajiv, please bring your Physics book to school tomorrow. "
Begin: (Ramesh ....)

(d) The heavy showers of rain revived the plants.
Use: (...........by..................)

(e) Sushil's attitude towards work has always puzzled me.
End: (..........................towards work.)

(ii) In the following sentences, replace the **INCORRECT** underlined words to make the sentences more meaningful and grammatically correct. (Do not copy the sentence) (5)

(a) She turned up the offer to work at the factory.

(b) To everyone's surprise, he turned out at the party.

(c) He broke through in the middle of his speech at the function.

(d) The burglars broke in the house when the family was away.

(e) He agreed to carry with the manager's orders.

(f) Sita's daughter carried through the family business when Sita went abroad.

(g) He ran out from home at the age of ten.

(h) I came with my old friend in the market place.

(i) Her aunt looks to her aging grandparents.

(j) The principal looks in matters of complaint from teachers and students.

(iii) Fill in the blanks in the passage given below with appropriate form of the verb given in brackets. Do not write the passage but write the verbs in correct order. (5)

One day, I ...... **(1)** (be) in the lunch line and saw a pile of apples. The Teacher-in-Charge ...... **(2)** (stare) at me and said, "Just .... **(3)** (take) one, God ...... **(4)** (watch)' So, I ...... **(5)** (take) an apple and the line ...... **(6)** (move) along. At the next table, there .... **(7)** (be) a pile of chocolate chip cookies. I .... **(8)** (not know) what to do. "Psst," the kid behind me .... **(9)** (whisper), " .... **(10)** (take) all you want. God's watching the apples."

Question 4.

Read the passage given below and answer the questions (i), (ii) and (iii) that follow.

(1) To be encumbered with a corpse is to be in a difficult position. True, any doctor, even one just out of medical school, would have been able to diagnose the cause of death. The man had died of heart failure or what the doctors call cardiac **arrest**. The cause of his heart having stopped pumping blood was that someone had slid a sharp sliver of steel between his ribs just far enough to penetrate the great muscle of the heart and to cause a serious and irreversible leakage of blood so that it stopped beating. Cardiac arrest, as I said.

(2) I wasn't too anxious to find a doctor because the knife was mine and the hilt had been in my hand when he died. I stood on the open road with the body at my feet and I was scared, so scared that the nausea rose in my throat to choke me. This particular body had been a stranger - I had never seen him before in my life.

(3) I was unarmed, if you accept the 'sgian dubh'-the black knife- which I always carry. The 'sgian dubh' is a much underrated weapon. Mine is at least a hundred and fifty years old. The ebony handle is ribbed on one side to give a good grip, 'but smooth on the other side so it **draws** clear without catching; the blade is less than four inches long; the stone **set** in the handle balances the knife so that it makes a superlative throwing weapon. I carry it in a flat sheath in my left sock.

(4) This is how it had happened.

(5) A little after I had driven out of the city, I saw a car ahead, pulled off the road and a man waving the universally recognised distress signal of the stranded motorist. It turned out, quite naturally, that there was something wrong with his car and he couldn't get it to move. I got out, walked over to his car and peered at the exposed engine.

(6) He didn't use the gun straight away. He first tried to take a swipe at me with a well- designed little club. I turned my head and saw his upraised arm and dodged sideways. If the club had connected with my skull it would have jarred my brains loose, instead it hit my shoulder and my whole arm went numb.

(7) I hopped back and groped for the 'sgian dubh' as I went. Fortunately it's a left-handed weapon which was just as well because my right arm wasn't going to be of any use.

(8) He came for me again but when he saw the knife he hesitated. He dropped the club and dipped his hand beneath his jacket and it was my turn to hesitate. But his club had a leather wrist loop and the dangling weapon spoilt his draw and I jumped him just as the pistol came out.

(9) I didn't stab him. He swung around and ran straight into the blade. He sagged against me with a look of surprise on his face. Then he went down at my feet and the knife came free.

(10) So there I was on a lonely road with a newly created corpse at my feet and a knife in my hand, a bad taste in my mouth and a frozen brain.

(11) From the time I had got out of my car to the moment of death had been less than two minutes.

(Adapted from** Running Blind **by Desmond Bagley)

SP-09

(i) (a) Find a single word from the passage that will exactly replace the underlined word or words in the following sentences. (3)

(1) The doctor explained that the new medication was especially designed for related to heart matter.

(2) The gardener carefully removed the cover of the blade before starting the lawnmower.

(3) After the accident he was temporarily deprived of sensation in his legs.

(b) For each of the words given below, choose the correct sentence that uses the same word unchanged in spelling, but with a different meaning from that it carries in the passage. (3)

(1) arrest (line 3)

(a) News of his death due to cardiac arrest caused a sensation after murder speculations.

(b) Following the coup, parliamentary leaders were put under house arrest.

(c) The organisation is working to arrest my mother's attention.

(d) Both (b) and (c)

(2) draws (line 14)

(a) The novelist draws heavily on her personal experiences.
(b) He draws his gun and points it in my direction.
(c) After stabbing the person, he draws his dagger towards himself.
(d) I can draw the skewer from the cheese without ruining it.

(3) set (line 14)

(a) Mother asked me to tear the cloth with my club so that she could use it.
(b) He drew out his club as soon as he saw various members of their rival group coming towards his him.
(c) Ratan had decided to join the Country Club after he found out the various benefits it offers.
(d) Abhishek had bought a new club as his old one broke off during a fight.

(ii) Answer the following questions in your own words as briefly as possible.

(a) How did the stranger die? (2)
(b) Why did the narrator stop his car and get out? (2)
(c) Describe the narrator's weapon. (2)

(iii) Describe the incident of killing of the stranger in not more than 100 words (Paragraphs 5 to 9). Failure to keep within the word limit will be penalised. (8)

Answers *in Topper's Style*

1. (i) I normally detest travelling by bus not because it is uncomfortable but because it gives me a feeling of claustrophobia. However, last month I had to go through this ordeal on being summoned by my uncle to Delhi. I had no other option as the travel decision was made last minute and no other mode of travel was available at an affordable price. The visit was in connection with my long pending Visa application. Thus, the matter was urgent and I had to reach Delhi by the next day to complete the formalities. With extreme dejection, I decided to take the bus.

As I reached the bus station, I saw a huge queue at the ticket counter as expected. Nestling my briefcase between my legs, I stood in the queue. The station was filling with people. Some were sitting on benches or on the floor, while still others lay asleep with bags under their head, prepared for an eternal wait. An occasional cow or dog would make a detour of the place, in search of eatables thrown by passengers. They were also bold enough to nibble at the bags. I hated to find myself amidst this filth. I nudged along in the queue which was advancing at a snail's pace. There was an occasional display of temper as people tried to jump the queue, which made the nudging and jostling even more unpleasant.

Just then, a person standing a little distance from me cried out that his pocket had been picked. He immediately collared the person pushing him, accusing him of the offence. I instinctively felt for my purse and was relieved to find it intact. By now, the fight had turned into a free for all, with allegations and counter allegations. Fortunately, a constable arrived on the scene and took both the warring parties aside. On checking the person of the accused, the stolen purse was found. While the public wanted to teach the pickpocket a lesson, the constable handled the situation with tact and led the culprit away in handcuffs.

As the commotion subsided, the queue for the bus-ticket moved and I could finally buy one for myself. Clutching the ticket in my hand, I looked around for a place to sit and wait for the bus I had to take. Seeing none, I placed my briefcase near a tea stall and sipped the hot tea. I felt relieved after the nerve wrecking experience I had just gone through. However, this relief was short lived.

As soon as the bus arrived, people rushed toward it. I also collected my wits and scrambled towards it. After a lot of pushing and jostling, I found myself in the bus. Exhausted, I thankfully sat on the first vacant seat which came my way. After about half an hour, the bus finally pulled out of the station. While dozing off to sleep, I made a mental note of never undertaking a long journey by bus, which leaves one weary even before the journey begins.

(ii) Travelling has been my father's longtime passion that I had found soon after I gained my mind and senses. He finds exploring unfamiliar places, meeting new people and getting to know different cultures exceptionally inspiring. Therefore, by the age of twelve, I had already been to many exotic places including Turkey, Russia, Thailand, Japan, Egypt, Malaysia, New Zealand, Australia and Cuba. All of these trips had fuelled the same passion within me as I started to wait eagerly to the trips.

Recently, my father had to go to Ukraine for work. He wanted to take us with him and since my younger brother and I had holidays during that period, the whole family went for the trip. I did not know what to expect from Ukraine since I knew little about it. But, somehow I knew that it would be an intriguing experience due to the spontaneous nature of my travel. Now, there is one thing I hate- to already explore the place over the internet. I feel that it ruins the wonders of exploring the place. So, with much excitement, I looked forward to the trip. Ukraine turned out to be completely different from any place I had visited so far. Kyiv, the capital city, appeared unexpectedly well-groomed, green and wealthy. The various bridges across the Dnipro River, a large number of outstanding parks, a couple of botanical gardens and flowers everywhere we went kept us mesmerised the entire time.

We travelled to Lviv – a wonderful medieval city with 800-year-old castles, Gothic catholic churches and palaces, flowers at every corner and on every window sill and original block pavement streets of the Old City. Lviv is a magical city which fueled me with inspiration to see the rest of the country.

Next, we went to Zaporizhzhia (quite a tongue twister). The city is built on two banks of the Dnipro River and has an island in the middle – Khortytsia – the biggest river island in the world.

The city itself seemed to me to be still Soviet-like in its spirit and atmosphere, so it was quite interesting to take photos of the famous dam with the huge Lenin statue pointing at it and the factories that were once the pride of the USSR and amazingly, still successfully functioning for export purposes nowadays.

Ukraine was a true discovery for me. If you should ask me what place I can recommend to those avid and bored travellers who seem to have seen it all, I would say without a second of hesitation: "Go to Ukraine! Whatever you will expect this will still amaze and astonish you."

(iii)

For the Motion

It is a universal fact that each one of us wants to join the biggest and the most prestigious of colleges in hopes of getting a highly paid job and a successful career. While science students aim for the IITs or AIIMS, literature students aspire to study at JNU or DU. Also, most commerce students opt for CAT preparations for IIMs while they partake their graduation degrees.

In today's world, career options are innumerable and the stakes are high. Hence, every student aims to join a reputed college or university not merely for the faculty or the infrastructure, but also for the exposure they will get through campus recruitment drives that include internship opportunities and mentoring from the best people/leaders in the field. With world class infrastructure, 24/7 facilities, employment opportunities in the colleges itself, the students are bound to get the practical skills and experience that is essential today in the job market. Reputed and top-notch universities guarantee a good teaching atmosphere, a well built infrastructure alongwith well-qualified teachers. Teachers in such institutions not only promote an effective learning but also act as guides and mentors students helping them in their future endeavours. The worldwide reputation of top-notch institutions also helps a student acquire a good paying well- settled job. Every year, during the time when placement drives are organised in colleges, we hear about great packages and lifestyles being offered to students from these elite universities. When the start of the career is elite, the future progression is bound to grow into more success. Hence, we often find students looking for admissions in such elite and good universities.

Against the Motion

"The road to success cannot be a spoon-feeding process. It can only be created by your hard work." Almost every student has the dream of getting into top-notch institutes for which they work hard. We have aspirants from every field, whether it be Science or Commerce or Arts. Some aspire to become engineers, doctors, entrepreneurs, designers, IAS/IFS Officers and what not. We all work hard to get the best percentage in 12th or an excellent All India Rank in competitive exams so that we can make our way to the renowned institutes. We all have a perception that if we get into top-notch institutes then our career is secured. Well, to some extent, it can be satisfactory to say that top-notch institutes open doors to various opportunities which can lead to having a successful career.

But no institution will guarantee you a safe and successful career. If it was true then, no student from a normal college could even have the chance of getting placed in their dream company with high salary package. Hence, we would find that no college prospectus will mention you a guarantee of a job or a profound career. Your success depends on your strategy mixed with your hard work, your efforts and your failures. Even if you get admission in one of the best universities, if you don't work hard there, then all your efforts will go in vain. Colleges focus on giving theoretical and bookish knowledge to the students while the practical skills and knowledge are dependent on the efforts that a student is willing to put into his/her career. Hence, even from the top notch universities, there are only a few students who get a successful career while others are average with average careers.

(iv) **Superstition**

We have often heard people stating the presence of an unseen power. Even though they can't define it precisely, they feel it is present and working. This is what gives rise to superstitions. They are unreasonable and irrational but they still exist all over the world. Superstition is a blind belief in the supernatural which is to say, a belief in the existence of forces or entities that do not conform to the laws of nature or a scientific understanding of the universe.

Man started to believe in superstitions when he got a feeling that humans are at the mercy of natural elements. Similarly, some superstitions were also created because of social values. As a result, people have been worshipping forces of nature for a long time. The Greeks and the Pagans used to worship elements of nature in the form of Gods and Goddesses. Same is the case with Indian tradition. People continue to worship the Sun, Moon, stars, planets, plants among many other thing believing that these things have the power to influence our lives.

India has a long history of superstitions. There are many superstitions which people in the country follow. You might have heard "it is because of the impact of some evil star or evil eye" and more when a disease overtakes or disaster strikes. In fact, ever since a long time, people still consider the number 13 to be unlucky. Similarly, salt spilling over the dinner table is also considered an ill-omen. In today's world, even in the age of rapid advancement of science and technology, people are afraid like their forefathers living in the caves and connect their misfortunes with mysterious and unknown forces. Such a state of mind always gives rise to various superstitions.

Firm beliefs in charms, supernatural powers, ghosts, goblins, witches and evil spirits have their deep roots in superstitions. It is vile as it deprives us of self-confidence, self-control, rationality, farsightedness, etc. by weakening our will power and spirit. It results from ignorance and irrational fear. This is the age of reason, science and technology yet many primitive superstitions continue endlessly. If we look at it closely, there is no logic as such behind superstitions. However, they have grown age-old and despite all the scientific advancement, they are not going anywhere soon.

(v) **Experience is the Best Teacher**

"Experience is a hard teacher because it gives the test first, the lesson afterwards," said Vernon Sanders Law. Indeed, lessons learnt through personal experience leave an indelible mark on our mind which are invaluable and lasting. Like a good teacher, the lessons learned from experience are very thorough and one can ignore it to one's own peril. Experiences could be good, like helping a person in need or bad like losing money on a risky investment. The important thing is the learning that we get from them. One gains from good experience and steers clear from harmful ones.

One is always heard saying that when an individual experiences a situation then only he/she will understand the lesson or morals. Telling a child not to play with a match box would probably have no impact on him but once he hurts or burns himself with the matchstick, he will never in his lifetime play with the match box. Learning from personal experience is surely more lasting and valuable than following the advice of others or reading about them from books or periodicals.

However, wise men learn from the experiences of others like parents, teachers or an elder. They also profit from books that are a virtual treasure house of knowledge and experience of great men. Acclaiming the importance of books, Francis Bacon said, "Some books are to be tasted, others swallowed and some few to be chewed and digested." Such books like the biographies of great statesmen, proverbs and folklore are a gold mine of knowledge and experience which enrich our lives. Life is one great journey of learning and experience is its best teacher. We learn the virtue of patience and forbearance when faced with adversity, courage in the face of danger and wisdom from mistakes. In this short span of life, one should not only learn from one's own experience but should also profit from the experience of others. This would save us from many pitfalls of life.

(vi) **The Box of Memories**

In a quiet attic, surrounded by dust, Rahul sat with a small, worn box in his lap. He had found it while sorting through his grandmother's belongings after she passed away. The box belonged to her, and Rahul hesitated before opening it. With a deep breath, Rahul lifted the lid. Inside were yellowed letters, black-and-white photos, and small trinkets. He found a photo of his grandmother as a young woman, smiling brightly in front of a quaint house. Her joy seemed to leap from the picture. Rahul imagined her laughter.

As he looked deeper in the box, he found everything from his birthday cards to his photos as a small baby. He teared up imagining his grandmother preserving all his memories inside a box. There were pressed flowers he had bought for her and the small locket he had given her a few years back. The box was a sweet torture reminding of all the happy shared memories while also making him realise that all there was left now were memories. Forever keeping one part of his grandmother with him. He was filled with the bittersweet appreciation for the life lost. He remained in the attic for a while longer soaking up all that it had to offer. He wanted to remain in peace with her grandmother's memories for a short while more. With the box in his arms he made the journey downstairs. He felt as if he carried the essence of his grandmother with him. The box for him was a symbol of love, life and the bond they shared.

2. (i) **Potholes Plague Indian Roads**

by Rahul, Staff Correspondent

Delhi, 12th August, 20XX Roads that were created with the aim to facilitate smooth travel between places are now covered with potholes. Today people dread commuting because of the poor conditions of our roads. As these holes increase people are left grappling with damaged vehicles, increased travel time and safety concerns.

These potholes have emerged as the biggest hassle of our daily lives. Motorists have to continuously deal with bent tires, damaged rims and poor suspension. Two-wheelers often move around these holes to avoid damage to their vehicles and cause more traffic congestion or worse, put themselves at risk of accidents. While on the other hand the car drivers face problems in their braking system. Even a car with the greatest suspension system has fallen prey to these potholes. Buyers have to restrict themselves from buying cars with little ground clearance as they are not suited for Indian roads. The cumulative effect of these challenges has led to frustration and a palpable sense of insecurity among residents.

Potholes pose a particularly daunting challenge for the elderly population in our community, significantly impacting their mobility and safety. For seniors with limited mobility or reliance on walking aids, navigating around potholes can be treacherous, increasing the risk of falls and injuries. Moreover, the uneven surfaces of potholed pavements can exacerbate joint pain and strain, further impeding their ability to move freely. Additionally, the stagnant rainwater collected in potholes not only contributes to road deterioration but also serves as a breeding ground for mosquitoes and other pests, potentially spreading diseases and posing health hazards to residents living in proximity to these neglected areas.

Although, the government and local authorities try to mend the broken roads every monsoon and have significantly elevated the standard of Indian roads, it is not enough. People are still troubled by these large craters and the disturbances it causes in their daily lives. It is also important to note that a collaborative effort is needed in this war against potholes.

(ii) **Proposal for Setting Up Culinary Club**

Heading The students will be able to learn practical skills which will help them throughout life. Setting up a culinary club in the school will help students to explore their talents.

Objectives To provide an environment for students to socialise, be creative, learn cooking skills and have fun and to inspire others to pursue their culinary dreams, we propose to setup the Culinary Club.

List of Measures

- To prepare a grocery list and divide it among the group members and designate one principal shopper to get all the ingredients.
- To choose tasty, nutritious recipes for the students and teachers during culinary club presentation. Members will also participate in cooking meals for fund raising events.
- The club membership will be open for all Classes from VII to X. The club membership has been set ₹ 200 per head per year.
- The club will be supervised by Ms Ranjana and Chef Sujit Singh will pay visit every Friday.

The classes will take place once a week after school from 2:00 to 4:00 pm in the school hall. We hope that this proposal will be accepted so that the Culinary Club can be setup as soon as possible.

3. (i) (a) No other girl in the class is as beautiful as Ashita.

(b) Hardly had she reached home, when she learnt that she had to leave for London.

(c) Ramesh requested Rajiv to bring his physics book to the school the next day.

(d) The plants were revived by the heavy showers of rain.

(e) I have always been puzzled by Sushil's attitude towards work.

(ii) (a) down (b) up (c) down
(d) into (e) out (f) on
(g) away (h) across (i) after
(j) into

(iii) 1. was 2. stared 3. take
4. is watching 5. took 6. moved
7. was 8. did not know 9. whispered
10. take

4. (i) (a) (1) cardiac (2) sheath (3) numb

(b) (1) (d) Both (b) and (c)

(2) (a) The novelist draws heavily on her personal experiences.

(3) (c) Ratan had decided to join the Country Club after he found out the various benefits if offers.

(ii) (a) The stranger died of cardiac arrest soon after he had been hit with a steel knife that the narrator used to defend himself from the stranger's assault.

(b) The narrator stopped his car and got out on seeing a man near his car giving a signal of distress as there was something wrong with the car.

(c) The narrator's weapon was a black knife, which he called 'Sgian Dubh'. It was a left handed weapon with ebony handle ribbed on one side to give a good grip. The other side had a smooth blade which was four inches long. It also had stone set in the handle which balanced the knife to make it an excellent throwing weapon.

(iii) As the narrator drove out of the city, he saw a car ahead and a man waving a signal of distress as something was wrong with his car. But, no sooner did the narrator approach him than he was attacked with a short club which hit him on his shoulder. The narrator groped for his knife at which the stranger hesitated. However, before the stranger could execute his plan of shooting the narrator with the pistol, the former swung round and ran straight into the blade. He sagged down against the narrator and was no more, as the narrator drew out the knife.

SQP Code : **PB-10/10** Series ***i*-Succeed 10-25/10** Roll No.

Sample Question Paper 10

English Language 12th (Code 801)

General Instructions

1. You are allowed additional 15 minutes for only reading the question paper.
2. You must NOT start writing during reading time.
3. It has four questions in all.
4. Answer all questions.
5. You are advised to spend not more than 45 minutes on Question 1, 55 minutes on Question 2, 30 minutes on Question 3 and 50 minutes on Question 4.
6. You should begin each answer on a fresh page.
7. The intended marks for questions are given in brackets [ ].

Time : 3 Hrs.

Max. Marks : 80

Question 1.

Write a composition (in approximately 400-450 words) on any one of the following subjects. (20)

(You are reminded that you will be rewarded for orderly and coherent presentation of material, use of appropriate style and general accuracy of spelling, punctuation and grammar.)

(i) Describe the scene at a busy railway station during the holiday season when your uncle saved a young boy.

(ii) You are of forgetful nature. Once you bought a lottery ticket and kept it safely. Later you were informed that you have won the first prize on your lottery ticket. But, where was the lottery ticket? Narrate how you managed to find out the lottery ticket.

(iii) "Rising prices can be controlled only by the government." Write **for** or **against** the topic.

(iv) Qualities needed for success

(v) 'Uneasy lies the head that wears the crown.' Express your views on the statement.

(vi) Write an original short story that begins with the words "It was raining hard that night. In my hurry to get into the house, I didn't notice the black car parked across the road, I realised something was wrong when...... ."

Question 2.

(i) Recently, you were a judge at a dance-based reality show on T.V. You noticed that the dances, as shown on T.V., seemed to be a mix of gymnastics and P.T. exercises. Write a report on the event along with your comment in about 300 words. You can use the following clues and add relevant details as well (15)

Dance as expression- rich culture of dance in India- unlike Western dance forms- visit to reality show- lack of traditional dance forms- need for revival- need of specific reality shows.

(ii) As the head of the Students' Wing of the RWA of your colony, you have been given the responsibility of organising a cultural programme in your colony on the occasion of Gandhi Jayanti. Write a proposal, in about 150 words, stating the steps you would take to effectively organise this event. (10)

Question 3.

Answer sections **(i)**, **(ii)** and **(iii)**

(i) Rewrite the following sentences according to the instructions given after each of them in the brackets. (5)

(a) I: Rahul can buy a car if he gets a promotion
Begin: (Unless ....)

(b) I : There are only a few apples left on the tree.
Use: (...............hardly.....................)

(c) I : This fact is too evident to require proof.
Use: (.......... so ....does not.....................)

(d) I : Only a rich man like Mr. Baruah can live such a luxurious life.
Begin: (None but ....)

(e) I : He's the funniest man I've ever met.
End: (.................. funnier than him.)

(ii) In the following sentences replace the **INCORRECT** underlined words to make the sentence meaningful and grammatically correct. (Do not copy the sentence) (5)

(a) The new supervisor is not very popular <u>in</u> her juniors.
(b) Most people are known <u>for</u> the company they keep.
(c) The manager impressed <u>over</u> his subordinates the need for more sales.
(d) Bamana was so sick after the party, that the doctor had to be called <u>over.</u>
(e) A cholera epidemic has broken <u>through</u> in the state.
(f) Conviction will carry you <u>from</u> difficult times.
(g) Jakob is very good <u>to</u> repairing things.
(h) The lead runner was running so fast that the rest of the field couldn't keep <u>at</u> with him.
(i) We knew we were drifting <u>through</u> towards the dangerous rocks.
(j) All parents fear <u>by</u> their children.

SP-10

(iii) Fill in the blanks in the passage given below with the appropriate form of the verb given in brackets. Do not write the passage but write the verbs in correct order. (5)

After they ...... **(1)** (walk) for a while, they .... **(2)** (see) an isolated cottage. They .... **(3)** (peep) through the broken window, ... **(4)** (look) for someone who .... **(5)** (guide) them back to the main road. They .... **(6)** (find) that the cottage ...... **(7)** (be) covered with dirty, cobwebs ...... **(8)** (hang) across the roof and it .... **(9)** (seem) to be unoccupied. They .... **(10)** (be) disappointed.

Question 4.

Read the passage given below and answer the questions (i), (ii) and (iii) that follow.

Boyhood and Balance

(1) My eldest boy has just turned nine. One day not long after, he was on his way to the pool on his bike when he slammed on his brakes in front of me and did a really neat skid. He looked back and gave me his cheesy smile of satisfaction.

(2) Normally that little skid would have provoked a stern warning not to 'wear out your tyres.' I was always been taught to take care of my things and keep them in good **shape**. I've come to learn, though, that there is a difference between the natural course of wearing things out and trying to make things last at any price. The difference became acute to me one bright sunny day four years ago.

(3) My then five-year-old boy had spent a normal summer afternoon playing in the **park** and swimming at the neighbourhood pool. At his bath time that night, I noticed he had small red spots all over his body. Some kind of measles, I thought and called my wife to take a look. By pure chance, the next day he had an appointment with his pediatrician.

(4) Several tests (and long hours) later, the doctors figured my son had an illness called ITP (Idiopathic Thrombocytopenic Purpura), which causes your spleen to kill off your body's own blood-clotting platelets. If it got worse, he could bleed to death internally. Only time would tell whether it would get better on its own. You can imagine the fear that crept into our hearts.

(5) Three days into his stay at the hospital, I went to pick out a **present** for him. I reached for a yellow toy convertible (he loves cars). My hand hesitated. I knew that it wouldn't last long with a five-year-old boy. Then I thought to myself: So what if the doors break off and the wheels fall off. If those things happen, it will mean he is alive and well. I bought it in the hope that he would be well enough to play with it. He was thrilled to receive it and it helped him pass the week he spent at the hospital.

(6) I saw the car the other day, sitting on a shelf in his room. The wheels have fallen off, the doors are broken and all of the chrome has worn off. I see it and I smile to myself. My boy has been perfectly well these past four years and is full of vitality. His mysterious illness came and went.

(7) And I learned that things are things and can be replaced if necessary. If any one of my three boys happens to break something or wear it out playing with it, instead of chastising him for carelessness, I now prefer to celebrate his boyhood. The empty shell of what once was a nice car, the balding tyre of his new bike, the lost pieces of his Monopoly game, all bear witness to the fact that there lives a healthy, happy boy.

(8) Prudence and preservation have their place, as do experimentation and curiosity. In the end, it is my relationships with my sons and my wife that have real lasting power. I choose to celebrate our lives with these material losses.

(9) Besides, I used to skid my tyres the same way - just not in front of my dad.

*(**Adapted from** Elliot Van Egmond 'The Globe and Mail')*

(i) (a) Find a single word from the passage that will exactly replace the underlined word or words in the following sentences. (3)

(1) He slides down the stairs not caring if he gets hurt doing it.

(2) Her cautioness in planning the trip ensured that everything went smoothly without any unexpected surprises.

(3) She was very excited about the upcoming trip to Delhi with her friends.

(b) For each of the words given below, choose the correct sentence that uses the same word unchanged in spelling but with a different meaning from that it carries in the passage. (3)

(1) shape (line 5)

(a) He kept the blanket in great shape.
(b) They were asked to shape the pot with their hands.
(c) My friend saw the shape of my car and laughed.
(d) The mummy was in bad shape after being studied.

(2) park (line 9)

(a) You need to go to the nearby park if you want to find Mr. Suresh.
(b) Please do not run around as there are many dogs in the park.
(c) Do not park your vehicle here for this is handicap parking.
(d) I wrote a letter to the MCD for the maintenance of the park.

(3) present (line 18)

(a) There is no time like the present; so, complete the task now.
(b) She was present in the class when the teacher called out her name.
(c) I had to think a lot before buying her a present.
(d) Both (a) and (b)

(ii) Answer the following questions in your own words as briefly as possible.

(a) Why is the disease ITP so serious? (2)
(b) What is most important to the writer now? (2)
(c) What did the writer learn from his experience? (2)

(iii) Summarise the given passage in not more than 100 words. Failure to keep within the word limit will be penalised. (8)

Answers *in Topper's Style*

1. (i) Most of us often visit railway stations to travel or to receive or see off a friend or a relative. All of us would agree that the scene at a railway station is always attractive and colourful, full of diverse people and activities. There are people of various classes, regions and religions going about their tasks, either waiting to pick someone up or to board a train.

A railway station is a meeting place for all sorts of people. I have always found myself observing the scene of railway station whenever I visit it. However, there is one particular day at the railway station which shall stay with me forever. It was a normal day when I went to see off my uncle at the railway platform during the holiday season. The train had not arrived and so we had to wait for some time. As usual, I started to look here and there to pass my time, captivated by the usual hustle bustle. Everything seemed to be normal as one could expect - the vendors' shouting, the passengers' anxiety, the coolies handling the luggage of the passengers, etc.

Just then, an announcement was made wherein my uncle's train was coming to the platform. In a hurry, all the passengers started collecting their luggage. Suddenly, we all heard a cry. A small child had fallen on the track where the train was fast approaching. He had fallen due to the constant pushing of the passengers who were hurrying without paying any attention to their surroundings. The mother was on the platform trying to get her child up. My uncle hurried to the child and jumped on the tracks. He got the boy and was trying to climb upstairs while a dread filled me. In a fit of adrenaline, I hurried to my uncle and started pulling him up. I hoped the train would see us and stop or would take time enough to get my uncle and the child to safety.

By now, everyone had come to aid. They were all pulling my uncle up and were successful in doing so. They sat my uncle and the child down and provided first aid to them. The entire crowd at the station had surrounded my uncle and was applauding him.

I was sitting with my uncle checking upon him while people began dispersing when the hoot of the train was heard nearby. People were again collecting their luggage but now with more attention. As the train stopped on the platform, people crowded the gates and started looking for their coaches as the railway station filled up again with its busy glory.

(ii) The clerk Mithun who had given me or had rather persuaded me to buy a lottery ticket came running to me one day. "Sir", he exclaimed, "take out your lottery ticket, if I remember your lottery number correctly, you may have won the lottery prize worth Rupees 5 crores." I had been thinking about the next advert we were to make so unconsciously I scrabbled around, "Lottery, what lottery ticket?" He was shocked. He reminded me that a few days back, he had persuaded me to buy a lottery ticket of Billboard State Lotteries. He had also asked me to keep it safely. However, I did not remember anything about the lottery ticket.

He asked me to go home and search for the ticket. As he informed me, he was to get 5 lakh if I would claim my prize money of 5 crores. Irritated by his constant poking, I closed my shop and went home along with him to look for the ticket.

I tried to recall where I could have kept it but just could not think of any place. I reached home and rang up my wife to come home immediately as Mithun was hovering over the ticket and expected the money. He was so confident and excited at the prospect that I myself had started thinking about the money now, if perhaps I had won. Meanwhile, I tried to search the lottery ticket in my cupboard. I took out all my diaries as sometimes I used to keep important papers in them. But, the ticket could not be traced.

I searched all possible places-my study table, drawer, folders, between the files but there was no trace of it. My wife came alarmed at why she was called so urgently from office. When I told her about the lottery ticket, she told me that I had indeed given her the ticket but could not recall where it was kept. For three hours, we searched all the possible places, looking nervous and dejected at the thought whether we had thrown away the lottery ticket and now would not be able to claim the prize.

Suddenly, a smile came on my wife's face as she remembered that she had given the lottery ticket to our son to keep it safely. We immediately rang up our son who had gone out with his friends. He confirmed to our delight that the ticket was with him and rushed home. What a relief it was to have found it finally! I had lost all hopes of claiming the money as the ticket was not traceable at all, but now we all were happy as a millionaire.

(iii)

For the Motion

The world today is faced with many crises which afflict mankind and deprive them of getting even the basic necessities of life. In this light, we may blame poverty and over population to be the root cause and it surely is. But, in doing so, we often ignore the reality of why the numbers of those who are poor is rapidly increasing. The answer is inflation or a steep rise in the price of essential commodities.

The problem of rising prices is one of the major problems our country is facing in the present times. The soaring prices of essential consumer products such as grains, vegetables, cooking oil, etc. had been the cause of the many woes that the common people of the country face today. Those who are poor are already in the worst state but those, who used to earn enough for food and shelter, are now reaching a state of dismal poverty. With less income and more spending, they cannot afford one or the other basic need of life. The middle income earners are, thus, becoming poor while the poor are becoming poorer.

Any solution, then, to the problem of price rise is two-fold, to check the rising prices and to bring the prices down. Being the central power and administrative body of the nation, the government can play a vital role in this. First, the government must take some necessary actions to prevent prices of essential commodities from sky-rocketing. Stringent action should be taken against hoarders and black marketers who manipulate market prices and sell goods at double and even triple the rate. The government also needs to review import and export of all essential commodities on a regular basis and impose controls on exports and ease restrictions on imports. Moreover, in adverse situations, subsidies can be utilise so that the prices can be kept low.

Inflation can be controlled to a large extent if the government gives full freedom to producers and sellers to sell their product anywhere in India without any restriction and ensure free movement of the produce without taxation. Though our governments have often talked about checking inflation, it has never outlined a confirmatory strategy in this regard. Facilities such as infrastructure, relaxation and subsides are in the hands of the government and, if the government takes concrete measures to control it, then the real welfare of the masses can be ensured.

Against the Motion

While I agree that rising prices are the cause of all the woe's faced by our country today, I beg to disagree with the belief that only government has the power to control it. What is even more tragic of our times is that we have an opposition which seems to have a myopic view on all issues and wants to blame the government for everything. Even an attempt to say that "Rising prices can only be controlled by the government" is a reflection of lack of information and understanding of market economics.

An in-depth understanding of how economies work would reveal that it is not solely in the government's hands to control the prices of goods. One of the major factors for increasing prices is the rapid growth of population coupled with increase in income of only some part of the population. In other words, while the increase in population has led to an increase in demand for goods and services, income of the population had not increased accordingly. This, in addition to less production of goods creates a gap in demand and supply, which results in rise in price levels of all commodities. As the price level of the basic necessities increases, the income which earlier was sufficient for a family of 4 now becomes less for the same family. The family can now afford only some of the basic necessities of life.

Besides these factors, a major cause of inflation is hoarding and black marketing of essential goods. The prices of onions and pulses are an example. One can also look at the COVID pandemic to see how the price of a product is controlled by such hoarders. One can also not forget natural causes like weather which have a huge impact on availability of goods. Lack of availability again leads to inflation.

The imbalance created by inflation is not under the control of only the government. Thus, any act by the government may fall in void if all of us don't come together to initiate change in the factors stated above. Thus, I cling to my view that the problem of rising prices cannot be controlled by the government alone. We all need to come together and work towards the cause.

(iv) **Qualities Needed for Success**

"If you wish to succeed in life, make perseverance your bosom friend, experience your wise counsellor, caution your elder brother and hope your guardian genius," said Joseph Addison.

These are indeed some basic qualities required to be successful in life. People possessing these qualities are successful in whatever they do, while others bear the fear of failure in almost all activities they indulge in. Success, therefore, does not come naturally. Behind it are innumerable qualities and values like perseverance, experience, caution and a never-say-no attitude that foster it.

Success is ninety nine per cent perspiration and one percent inspiration. There are many stories of people who achieved great success by sheer force of hard work and determination. People like Lal Bahadur Shastri rose from very humble beginnings to reach the level of respect and adulation that was received by them. Some of the richest businessmen like Dhirubhai Ambani and Bill Gates also came from a very humble background. However, their zeal and enthusiasm made them establish great business empires.

Such great men also possess a keen and sharp mind and a clear vision of the goal they want to achieve in life besides dedication and perseverance. They also had the courage of conviction to move away from the beaten track and blaze a new trail for others to follow.

Besides the above qualities, one must exercise caution and patience in dealing with problems. Rushing from one action to another without thinking of its implication gets one nowhere. There is always a need to think about the problem, seek the views of experts, elders and peers and use past experiences, before coming to a decision. All decisions must be taken consciously with patience as all things take time to show results.

The last but not the least prerequisite is a positive attitude and mindset. This enables one to have an optimistic approach to problems and seek opportunities in them. Such a person is not easily disheartened and his perseverance pays off in the long run. Agreeably, there is no short cut to success and it does not come by chance. One has to assiduously work for it, with dedication and perseverance. This is beautifully presented in the words of H.W. Longfellow, 'Life's battle does not always go, to the stronger and the fastest man, But sooner or later the man who wins is the man who thinks he can'.

(v) Authority and power are always followed by a lot of responsibility. The charm of authority is inviting, but the eternal liability attached with it makes everything bothersome. This is exactly what the proverb 'Uneasy lies the head that wears the crown' tries to propagate.

The crown or a powerful position has always been symbolic of the topmost authority. Whenever we think about our kings and leaders, we think about luxury and comfort. We think that such a dignitary must have a happy and carefree life. But such outward appearances are very deceptive. The crown brings with itself unlimited responsibilities, innumerable worries and tensions which makes those who are crowned anxious and stressed. What seems a bed of roses to us, is actually a bed of thorns for the crowned.

Time and again, the saying has proved to be true. Yudhishthira– the eldest of the five Pandavas in the *Mahabharata,* Nelson Mandela, Mahatma Gandhi, Emperor Ashoka and all other powerful leaders of human history have shown that the one in power is always apprehensive. They show that the head of a state always needs to be alert and cautious against conspiracies. He/she not only has to look after the affairs of the government and the welfare of the people but also has to oversee the law and order in the country. At the same time, he/she must also maintain peace at the borders of the country, keep his/her opponent in check and listen to public criticism. While taking care of his/her duties, he/she has to be an ideal person and a model whom people are supposed to follow.

Just like a king and the head of a state, the principal of an institution has to ensure discipline and create a conducive atmosphere for learning. He/she not only keeps a vigilant eye on teachers and students but also handles all grievances. Similarly, the head of the family also has to worry about the welfare of his/her family. Even in the field of sports, the onus of loss and victory falls upon the captain. The burden of many responsibilities makes one lose all peace of mind while everyone is sleeping peacefully.

The person who controls power and authority always has to strive hard to achieve stability, solidarity and prosperity of his/her subjects. The security, basic needs, justice and general well-being of the masses are his/her duty. Such a person is at all times concerned with the well-being of others. The sense of duty is such a burden that he/she can neither ignore it nor avoid it. He/she is, therefore, bound to forget all about himself/ herself and devote heart and soul to do his/her best for them.

To lead a bunch of people is deemed prestigious. But, this prestige comes at the cost of comfort and peace. Hence, a more superior position held by an individual means more anxieties and the less chances for personal comforts.

(vi) **A Pleasant Surprise**

It was raining hard that night. In a hurry to get into the house, I didn't notice the black car parked across the road, I realised something was wrong when I heard strange muffled voices coming from inside the car. Was I being followed? Were there some robbers sitting inside that car ready to rob any one of the houses? Who exactly was sitting in the car and why were they parked here?

I was really terrified when suddenly I saw a man or should I say a dark hidden figure, get out of the car. The man, as I had guessed, was formally dressed in black and looked sinister. While I was trying to observe him, he started walking towards me. 'He must've noticed me', I thought while I was shivering from the chill in the rain and most probably because I was wet. So, I ran to the door of my house. As soon as I tried to ring the bell of the house that man called out 'Excuse me'.

I was terrified at that man's call and wanted to run away but could not. The man asked me if I knew a mechanic nearby as he was a stranger in this city and heading towards Delhi where his mother was admitted in a hospital. I was still not sure whether I should trust that man but at the same time my father opened the door.

I just decided to go inside the house when my father happened to have a glance at that stranger. Suddenly, my father screamed with excitement "Oh Shreekant, how come you are here. You had disappeared suddenly". That man looked at my father and came running towards him and screamed "Oh Pulkit, it is your house? You are settled in this city." My father asked him to come inside as the weather was really bad. I was totally confused as I didn't know the stranger and thought of him as evil but my father was meeting him like they had been friends for years.

My father introduced me to that man. He was his fellow classmate some 22 years back. After finishing college, they had not been in touch with each other. And now they had met accidently. My father was really excited upon meeting him. He called the mechanic to get his car repaired and invited that man to stay and rest till the rain stopped. So, initially what was scary for me, turned out to be a pleasant surprise for my father.

2. (i) **Dance Based Reality Show**

by Govind, Staff Correspondent

Dance is one of the most mesmerising ways of expressing oneself. This is why India has a very rich tradition of classical and folk dances. Our classical dance forms pay specific attention to expression and body language with its many mudras. The beauty that we ascribe to the Indian dance is because unlike any Western dance form, Indian dances take inspiration from the nature and, hence, are so full of life.

However, our media has started paying less attention to these beautiful traditional forms and focus on Western dance. Recently, I visited a dance based reality show on T.V. as a judge. Each of the participants of the show gave exceptional performance and I was mesmerised. Although the dance forms performed were amazing, I was saddened by the fact that the forms were generally Western with a mix of gymnastics and PT exercises. None of the contestants performed or specialised in the traditional Indian dance forms.

While I feel happy that we are expanding and bringing in new dance forms from outside, I also feel saddened by the fact that the traditional Indian dance forms are getting forgotten. I feel that starting a new reality show to promote and appreciate the Indian classical dances will make Indians understand its rich and divine values. Indians are well known for their culture and arts and, without them, its value is minimised.

It is high time Indian dances were brought under the spotlight once again. Since, the popularity and viewership of these reality shows are high. Indian dances will reach a large target audience who will soon realise that the classical and folk dance represents India's beautiful cultural legacy. Hence, they must be protected to revive the national spirit and stop the traditional dance forms from dying out.

(ii) **Proposal for Organising a Cultural Programme on the Occasion of Gandhi Jayanti**

Heading To organise a cultural programme for everyone so that children as well as adults can showcase their talents.

Objectives The cultural event would not only allow children and adults to enjoy the free day but would also sensitise everyone about the cultural importance of our nation. It would also foster a need to preserve the cultural heritage and art forms of the nation.

List of Measures

- The event will be held in the society premises with a centre stage being set up.
- Breakfast and lunch will be included in the event.
- The theme of the event will be Indian Tradition and Culture.
- Children as well as adults will be asked to prepare their performances on the selected theme.
- Award ceremony for the winners as well as the participants will be held.
- A painting and a poster making competition will be held for children.
- To successfully organise the event, a sum of ₹500 will be collected from each household.

We hope that the proposal will be accepted so that the Cleanliness Drive can be organised well.

3. (i) (a) Unless Rahul gets a promotion, he can't buy a car.
(b) There are hardly any apples left on the tree.
(c) This fact is so evident that it does not require proof.
(d) None but a rich man like Mr. Baruah can live such a luxurious life.
(e) I've never met a man funnier than him.

(ii) (a) among (b) by (c) upon (d) for
(e) out (f) through (g) at (h) up
(i) away (j) for

(iii) 1. walked 2. saw 3. peeped 4. looking
5. could guide 6. found 7. was 8. hung
9. seemed 10. were

4. (i) (a) (1) skid (2) prudence (3) thrilled
(b) (1) (b) They were asked to shape the pot with their hands.
(2) (c) Do not park your vehicle here for this is handicap parking.
(3) (d) Both (a) and (b)

(ii) (a) The disease ITP is serious because it causes patient's spleen to kill off his body's own blood-clotting platelets. If it becomes worse, the patient could bleed to death internally.
(b) The most important thing for the writer is his relationship with his sons and his wife. He had accepted that prudence and preservation are important. However, experimentation and curiousity are also important. So, he is going to celebrate his life, his relationships as well as the material losses.
(c) From his experience, the writer learnt that things can be easily replaced whenever necessary. The most important thing is to celebrate life and its little joys along with the relationships that empower us.

(iii) The writer compares his childhood with that of his children. He finds that there is a difference between the natural course of wearing things out and trying to make things last at any price. The contrast became clear to him when his five-year-old boy was admitted in the hospital for the treatment of ITP (Idiopathic Thrombocytopenic Purpura). The disease was serious but it disappeared mysteriously. The writer experimented with a toy car and it worked very well. The boy became perfectly well.